Madagascar

Cavendish
Square

New York

Published in 2018 by Cavendish Square Publishing, LLC
243 5th Avenue, Suite 136, New York, NY 10016
Copyright © 2018 by Cavendish Square Publishing, LLC

Third Edition

Library of Congress Cataloging-in-Publication Data

Names: Heale, Jay, author. | Latif, Zawiah Abdul, author. | Nevins, Debbie, author.
Title: Madagascar / Jay Heale, Zawiah Abdul Latif, Debbie Nevins.
Description: Third edition. | New York : Cavendish Square Publishing, 2018. |
Series: Cultures of the world (Third edition) | Includes bibliographical references and index. | Audience: Grades 5-8.
Identifiers: LCCN 2017041694 (print) | LCCN 2017042209 (ebook) | ISBN 9781502632425 (library bound : alk. paper) | ISBN 9781502632418 (ebook)
Subjects: LCSH: Madagascar--Juvenile literature.
Classification: LCC DT469.M26 (ebook) | LCC DT469.M26 H43 2017 (print) | DDC 969.1--dc23
LC record available at https://lccn.loc.gov/2017041694

Writers, Jay Heale, Zawiah Abdul Latif; Debbie Nevins, third edition
Editorial Director, third edition: David McNamara
Editor, third edition: Debbie Nevins
Art Director, third edition: Amy Greenan
Designer, third edition: Jessica Nevins
Picture Researcher, third edition: Jessica Nevins

PICTURE CREDITS

Cover: blickwinkel/Alamy Stock Photo
The photographs in this book are used with the permission of: p. 1 GUDKOV ANDREY/Shutterstock.com; p. 3, 18, 21, 86 Dennis van de Water/Shutterstock.com; p. 5, 77, 114 Dietmar Temps/Shutterstock.com; p. 6, 37, 38 RIJASOLO/AFP/Getty Images; p. 7 ANDREEA CAMPEANU/AFP/GettyImages; p. 8 AridOcean/Shutterstock.com; p. 10, 112 aaabbbccc/Shutterstock.com; p. 11, 53 Dudarev Mikhail/Shutterstock.com; p. 12 Nicolas Primola/Shutterstock.com; p. 13, 14, 24, 40, 44, 45, 64, 104 Pierre-Yves Babelon/Shutterstock.com; p. 15, 121 byvalet/Shutterstock.com; p. 16, 20 Anna Veselova/Shutterstock.com; p. 17 YuG/Shutterstock.com; p. 19, 124 Hajakely/Shutterstock.com; p. 22 reptiles4all/Shutterstock.com; p. 26 javarman/Shutterstock.com; p. 28 Chris Hellier/Corbis via Getty Images; p. 29 Bettmann/Getty Images; p. 30 Amin Mohamed/Camerapix/Keystone/Getty Images; p. 33 MONEY SHARMA/AFP/Getty Images; p. 34 anthony asael/Corbis via Getty Images; p. 39, 110, 116 ALEXANDER JOE/AFP/Getty Images; p. 42, 73 Muriel Lasure/Shutterstock.com; p. 46, 48, 76 Artush/Shutterstock.com; p. 47 Hugh Lansdown/Shutterstock.com; p. 50 Jan Bures/Shutterstock.com; p. 52 Raphael GAILLARDE/Gamma-Rapho via Getty Images; p. 54 LouieLea/Shutterstock.com; p. 56 Luis Marden/National Geographic/Getty Images; p. 58, 66 Anton_Ivanov/Shutterstock.com; p. 61 Insights/UIG via Getty Images; p. 62 Arterra/UIG via Getty Images; p. 63 Veronique DURRUTY/Gamma-Rapho via Getty Images; p. 68 Angela N Perryman/Shutterstock.com; p. 69, 70, 126 Damian Ryszawy/Shutterstock.com; p. 71 David Thyberg/Shutterstock.com; p. 78 Melanie Stetson Freeman/The Christian Science Monitor via Getty Images; p. 80 milosk50/Shutterstock.com; p. 82 Universal History Archive/UIG via Getty Images; p. 88 Saveoursmile (Hery Zo Rakotondramanana)/Wikimedia Commons/File:Famadihana reburial razana ancestor Madagascar.jpg/CC BY-SA 2.0; p. 92 David Evans/National Geographic/Getty Images; p. 93 Archive Photos/Getty Images; p. 94 KRISS75/Shutterstock.com; p. 95 ronemmons/Shutterstock.com; p. 98 Peter Wollinga/Shutterstock.com; p. 100 frank wouters/Wikimedia Commons/File:Aepyornis skeleton -Tsimbazaza Zoo, Madagascar-8a.jpg/CC BY 2.0; p. 102 DickDaniels/Wikimedia Commons/File:Sickle billed Vanga RWD.jpg/CC BY-SA 3.0; p. 103 Golden Brown/Shutterstock.com; p. 107 Aquintero82/Wikimedia Commons/File:Zafimaniry house.JPG; p. 108 Wolfgang Kaehler/LightRocket via Getty Images; p. 113 Henitsoa Rafalia/Anadolu Agency/Getty Images; p. 118 Aiky RATSIMANOHATRA/Shutterstock.com; p. 122 Pierre Jean Durieu/Shutterstock.com; p. 125 Jabin Botsford/The Washington Post via Getty Images; p. 127 Boaz Rottem/Alamy Stock Photo; p. 128 Kletr/Shutterstock.com; p. 129 Peter Bischoff/Getty Images; p. 130 Fanf/Shutterstock.com; p. 131 Claire Stout/Alamy Stock Photo.

PRECEDING PAGE

Like all lemurs, the ring-tailed lemur is endemic to Madagascar.

Printed in the United States of America

CONTENTS

MADAGASCAR TODAY

FOR THE PEOPLE OF MADAGASCAR, CALLED THE MALAGASY, there truly is "no place like home." It's not merely sentiment; it's a statement of fact. This island nation, which lies off the eastern coast of southern Africa, is unlike anywhere else on earth. Isolated from other land masses, and untouched by humans for thousands of years longer than most places, the island developed a staggering profusion of unique plants and animals.

However, as rich in beauty and biodiversity as it is, Madagascar is terribly poor in other ways. In fact, the Malagasy are among the world's most impoverished people. They themselves are an ethnically diverse people, with their genetic origins in Southeast Asia, Polynesia, India, Arabia, and East Africa. Culturally, too, they draw from these sources, as well as from France, which held Madagascar as a protectorate and colony from 1882 to 1958.

Linguistically, the people all speak the same language—also called Malagasy, though there two distinct dialects, each with its own variations. French and English are also official languages, though not universally spoken.

Police confront supporters of the opposition party Tiako I Madagasikara as they celebrate the party's fifteenth anniversary on July 8, 2017, despite a ban against the gathering.

Although DNA sampling has shown that all Malagasy display a mixed heritage of both Malaysian/Polynesian and African ancestry, there are nevertheless noticeable differences among them. The Merina people of the central highlands region tend to exhibit more Austronesian characteristics while the Fianarantsoa, or coastal people, are more African. The two groups tend to distrust each other, a cultural legacy that plays out in the nation's politics. Historically, the Merina had the higher social status, stemming from their history as rulers before the French colonial era. Africans, on the other hand, first came to the island as slaves of Arab traders. These outdated social hierarchies are unofficially maintained, which naturally leads to civil strife.

Politically, the Malagasy of all ethnicities have suffered from poor governing in the years since winning independence. They have been subject to dictatorships, coups, censorship and repression, corruption, and multiple rewrites of the constitution. All this recently came to a head during the so-called political crisis of 2009, which was marked by violence and demonstrations.

This political upheaval has had a disastrous effect on the nation's economy, and the poorest people—who are a majority—are the ones who suffer the most. Today, Madagascar is a precarious democratic state with a popularly-elected president and a prime minister, a legislature, and a multi-party system. Many international organizations are pouring billions of dollars into programs designed to help Madagascar pull itself up out the depths of poverty. However, political and civic stability is desperately needed for this to be successful.

In addition, a multitude of other problems stand in the way of progress. The island's beauty, tropical weather, beaches, and exceptional flora and fauna make it a natural draw for tourists—particularly for wildlife- and ecotourism. However, fewer than two hundred thousand visitors arrived in Madagascar in 2013, and of those, merely sixty thousand came mainly as tourists.

One big reason is that the infrastructure necessary to support a thriving tourism industry simply doesn't exist. Modern, well-paved highways are few, and utterly insufficient to support the sort of transportation systems that would help produce and serve a robust economy. Electricity, clean water, and sanitation facilities are likewise inadequate, not to mention such "luxuries" as air conditioning. In 2008, Madagascar had approximately 550 hotels, about 110 of which were classified as meeting international standards. Although some new hotels have been built since then, the nation still has a long way to go to cash in on this prime natural resource.

Magnificent scenery can be glimpsed behind a typical hotel in Anja, in southern Madagascar.

On the other hand, people looking for a challenging but authentic experience, without the commercialized sameness of some of the world's more crowded tourist attractions find the island to be a fascinating place to visit. However, such rugged sorts will never support the level of tourism that Madagascar needs to significantly impact its economy.

Madagascar is a land with a troubling history but with much promise for a better future. For the sake of the people, the animals, and the incredible land itself, the world can only hope this nation on the fourth-largest of earth's islands will realize its potential through peace, stability, and good fortune.

GEOGRAPHY

This relief map shows Madagascar's location to the east of the African continental mainland.

1

MADAGASCAR IS AN ISLAND NATION off the southeastern coast of Africa. It is usually considered a part of the African continent, though it is, in many ways, its own unique geographical place. About 88 million years ago, in the process of continental drift, this massive chunk broke away from what would become India. The land mass of India eventually crashed into Asia—forming the Himalayas in the process—but Madagascar remained marooned in the Indian Ocean, cut off from contact with any other body of land. As a result, more than 80 percent of its plants and animals are exclusive to the island. The island lies some 250 miles (400 kilometers) to the east of the African nation of Mozambique.

Madagascar is the fourth-largest island in the world, after Greenland, New Guinea, and Borneo. It has a landmass of 226,657 square miles (587,040 sq km), including its offshore islands. About

"Madagascar, I may announce to naturalists, is their promised land; it is there that nature seems to have retreated as into a private sanctuary, to work on different models from any she has used elsewhere: The most curious, the most marvellous forms can be found at every step...."
—Joseph Philibert Commerson, a French naturalist who visited the island in 1770

Terraced rice fields in the valleys of the Central Highlands attest to the people's Southeast Asian heritage.

1,000 miles (1,609 km) long, Madagascar is approximately twice the size of the state of Arizona and has about three times as many people. There are no particularly high mountains, but a high plateau, ranging in height from 2,450 to 4,430 feet (750 to 1,350 meters), runs down its north-south axis like a backbone.

Most of the 24.43 million Malagasy (the people of Madagascar) live on what they can produce from the land. The island is divided into twenty-two regions and six provinces—Anamalanga in the central highlands, Sofia to the northwest, Sava to the northeast, Diana on the northern tip, Atsimo-Andrefana on the southwest, and Vatovavy-Fitovinany on the southeast.

CENTRAL HIGHLANDS

The high plateau forming the spine of Madagascar is the land of the Merina, the most numerous, and once most powerful, of the Malagasy clans. It is still the most prosperous area in the country. Rolling hills form pastures for the humpback zebu cattle, while the valleys are terraced with rice fields. In the west, the hills turn bare and dry; in the east, forested slopes lead to the narrow coastal plain. At Périnet Reserve, reached by road from Antananarivo, there is a population of indri, the largest of the lemur species. Semiprecious stones such as jasper, rose quartz, sapphire, tourmaline, and amethyst are found in small quantities in the mountains. Snow is not uncommon on the highlands in the winter.

ANTANANARIVO

Surrounded by the twelve sacred hills of the Imerina plateau is Antananarivo (usually shortened to Tana), the capital of Madagascar. Meaning "city of the thousand" in Malagasy, it is a city of more than 1.4 million people. Not only is it by far Madagascar's largest city, it is also its administrative, communications, and economic center. The city sits 4,199 ft (1,280 m) above sea level, sprawling over a curving ridge, with a central square on one side and Lake Anosy on the other.

In the Upper Town lies the Presidential Palace, with government buildings clustered around it. Some of the better hotels, like the Colbert Hotel and the Radama Hotel, are in this area, as well as the tourist office that distributes free maps and advice.

The city of Antananarivo shines in the bright light of a sunny day.

THE ELEPHANT BIRD

The elephant bird was neither a fantasy creature nor a beast that disappeared with the dinosaurs. The Aepyornis maximus *was a large flightless bird that lived on Madagascar until its extinction sometime between the eleventh to seventeenth centuries (sources differ). It was the largest bird alive, about 9.8 feet (3 meters) tall and weighing some 880 pounds (400 kilograms). One egg could, theoretically at least, make an omelet big enough to feed more than one hundred people. Indeed, fossilized eggshell fragments found among the remains of ancient human fires suggest the eggs regularly provided meals for the people on the island. Though no one is certain what brought about the demise of the species, human hunting—of the bird itself or its eggs—seems a likely cause.*

The name "elephant bird" seems like a misnomer, given that elephants never existed on Madagacar. The name appears to originate with Marco Polo, the thirteenth-century Venetian explorer who, in 1298, wrote an account of a roc, a bird "strong enough to seize an elephant with its talons." While the roc is a mythological creature in Middle Eastern folklore, the "elephant bird" name somehow came mean Madagascar's very real, but now extinct, animal.

An illustration of the extinct elephant bird.

Higher, in the skyline, are the four towers of the Queen's Palace and the associated Royal Village, known as the Rova. Both the palace and the village were gutted by fire in November 1995, and all that remained were rows of arched windows gaping at the sky. Fortunately, many of the historic items that had been on display were saved from the fire. More than twenty years later, the palace is still undergoing restoration, but progress has been slow. On this higher ridge also stand several Catholic churches, four of them dedicated to Malagasy martyrs, and many schools.

THE SOUTH

The southern areas are a mixture of semidesert, coral-fringed beaches, nature reserves, scrub-covered hills, and the stark sandstone peaks of L'Isalo National Park. This is the driest part of Madagascar—a "spiny" desert where baobab, aloe, and spiky green octopus trees (similar to but unrelated to cactus) live in a tangle of thorny scrub. Large areas have been cleared to grow sisal, processed for cordage, which stand in pointy green rows in the red soil. The French introduced the prickly pear cactus from Mexico, and it is used as natural fencing and for feeding cattle.

Only 5 miles (8 km) east of this semidesert, separated by a mountain range, is a tropical east coast jungle and the breezy town of Tôlanaro. It is also known as Fort Dauphin, taking its name from the French-built fort there that now lies in ruins. Residents of the town prefer its Malagasy name, but most guidebooks retain the French colonial name. The town is built on a peninsula with a small harbor on one side, overlooked by the red-painted Palais de Justice. A large crucifix stands on a hill above the town. Hotels and restaurants in the area cater to the needs of tourists.

Sisal grows at a plantation near Tôlanaro.

Fragments of fossilized eggs belonging to the extinct "elephant bird," a giant flightless bird native to Madagascar, have been found in this region. Two popular nature reserves are the Berenty and Kaleta parks, which serve as a refuge for ringtail and brown lemurs, as well as the creamy-white sifaka lemurs and huge fruit bats. The tamarind gallery forest is found among the lush green undergrowth of the eastern coastal strip, also home to the rare three-cornered palm and the carnivorous pitcher plant.

THE EAST

The eastern part of Madagascar, with its almost straight coastline, is known as the Whale Highway because of the migrating humpback whales that gather offshore to breed. It is also nicknamed the Pirate Coast because of legends about the presence of pirates in the area in the past. An inland waterway, the Pangalanes Canal, runs parallel to the shore. This is 375-mile (603-km) chain of lakes and canals was once thronged with canoes carrying great loads of fruit and vegetables. Now it's clogged with reeds and water hyacinths, and used mainly for local fishing.

The Pangalanes Canal was built between 1896 and 1904, during the French colonial period, to provide safe passage for cargo boats.

The eastern shoreline is a fertile area drenched with tropical rains from December to March. It is also known as the Cyclone Coast, after the hurricanes that originate in the tropics. In 2017 Madagascar was hit by Cyclone Enawo, its strongest cyclone in thirteen years. Enawo packed winds in excess of 140 miles (225 km) per hour, the equivalent of a Category 4 hurricane. It claimed 81 lives (with another 18 missing), injured 180, and left more than 110,000 people homeless. Historically, the most destructive storm, Cyclone Gafilo, occurred in 2004. With winds reaching 160 mph (230 km/h), Gafilo left 237 dead, 181 missing, and hundreds of thousands homeless. These and many other devastating tropical storms, combined with centuries of slash-and-burn clearing of rain forests, have eroded the steep slopes of Madagascar's terrain, causing gaping red holes in the landscape known as *lavaka* (LA-vak).

Ships dock in the port of Toamasina.

Toamasina on the east coast is Madagascar's largest port, exporting sugar, coffee, cloves, and rice. It is connected to the capital by road, rail, and air. The town has a population of over 206,000 and is a popular holiday resort for residents.

Nosy Boraha, previously named Île Sainte-Marie (St. Mary's Island), farther north, is an island off the east coast that boasts the world's only pirate graveyard. Wind and rain have erased most of the carved inscriptions, but it's unlikely that any of the most infamous pirates of Madagascar are buried there.

The country's largest lake, Alaotra, was once in a wooded area. Then, as has happened throughout much of Madagascar, the trees were cut down to provide land for the cultivation of crops and grazing for cattle. The soil eroded and washed into the lake, which is now less than a third of its original size. The town of Ambatondrazaka once fronted the lake but is now 4.35 miles (7 km) from the water.

The baobab is sometimes described as an "upside-down tree" because it looks as if someone had plucked it from the earth and shoved it back in with its roots in the air. In

fact, it may be wrong to classify it as a tree at all because it is a succulent plant that stores water in its trunk. Unlike most trees, it does not die when the bark is stripped off. The bark is used to make fibrous cloth, baskets, strings for musical instruments, and waterproof hats. The lightweight wood is used for fishing floats and canoes. The leaves are eaten like spinach, the seeds provide oil, the empty seed husks are used as utensils, and the pulp makes a refreshing drink.

There are eight species of baobab in the world: six are found only in Madagascar, and the others in Africa and Australia. They can live for several thousand years, so many of the baobabs on Madagascar were alive long before humans arrived on the island. The impressive Avenue of the Baobabs stands near Morondava, and tourists often travel there to view two baobabs entwined like lovers.

High rainfall makes this the greenest part of the island. Cloves, vanilla, coffee, and fruit are grown for export, and rare orchids flourish. The ocean shoreline is picturesque, although swimmers have to be wary of sharks. Sometimes gold cups and coins are found washed up on the beach, fueling hopeful tales of buried pirate treasure.

THE NORTH

Much of northern Madagascar is cut off by the rugged Tsaratanana massif (mountain mass), which is the locale of extinct volcanic mountains, as well as the island's highest peak of 9,436 feet (2,876 m), Maromokotro. Differing altitudes of these mountains cause varied weather conditions, ranging from sporadic heavy rains to dry and cool periods.

The area around Antsiranana is dry, while the island-strewn coastline around Nosy Be in the west has higher rainfall. Antsiranana, which is also known as Diego-Suarez, has one of the finest deepwater harbors in the world. During its history, the port has accommodated slavers, pirates, a French naval base built in 1885, and the British during World War II. A legend tells of the existence of a seventeenth-century republic, Libertalia, founded there by pirates.

The stone formations of red tsingy seem to jut out of the ground, but were actually formed by erosion.

Local industries include shipbuilding, tuna fishing, salt extraction, and agriculture. Inland, there is Amber Mountain National Park, a volcanic massif covered with forest. Picturesque waterfalls with malachite kingfishers and varieties of bats attract tourists, while the dense trees conceal chameleons, orchids, and endangered species of lemur. Crocodiles live in the humid underground caves, and there are several species of shrimps, according to studies initiated by the World Wildlife Fund (WWF).

Farther south is Ankarana, an area of weirdly shaped, razor-sharp limestone pinnacles known as *tsingy* (TSING-i), meaning "spikes." Local communities, who have buried several of their kings in one of the caves there, consider the area sacred.

Nosy Be, meaning "big island," is a popular tourist destination. The increasing numbers of tourists pronounce this "NOSS-i BAY," but residents prefer "noosh BAY." Its setting of fertile greenery, vanilla plantations, and sweet-smelling yellow ylang-ylang blossoms, which are used to make perfume—combined with fine beaches and stunning marine life for those keen on snorkeling—make for a perfect holiday. There are expensive hotels catering to wealthy visitors and also low-priced ones for the budget conscious. The tourist atmosphere here, however, is not representative of Madagascar as a whole.

LEMURS

The ancestors of the lemurs on Madagascar may have drifted from the African mainland on logs. Without any large predators on the island, they evolved freely, and today there are varieties ranging from the mouse lemurs to giant, bearlike lemurs. Some species became extinct after man arrived on the island. The remaining sixty species and subspecies are constantly threatened by the slash-and-burn clearing of the forests.

Lemurs are not monkeys, although they are the closest living descendants of the common ancestor of the monkeys. Other survivors of this line are the bush babies of Africa. Monkeys are more clever than lemurs, which are more primitive and gentle primates. Lemurs live largely on fruit and insects. Their long noses give them a highly developed sense of smell. About half the thirty-three species are nocturnal, including the strangest of all, the aye-aye.

The aye-aye looks like a large-headed squirrel with bat's ears, a fox's tail, and tiny hands with a bony middle finger that it uses to dig for grubs or pick out the kernels from nuts.

Unfortunately, many superstitious Malagasy believe that the aye-aye bring bad luck. They fear that the "crooked finger" may point out the next person to die, so many aye-aye have been deliberately killed. Aye-aye have also incurred the anger of farmers because they have a sweet tooth and raid coconuts and sugarcane. There is a protected aye-aye reserve on the island of Nosy Mangabe.

Bemaraha Tsingy, Madagascar's largest nature reserve at 375,600 acres (152,000 hectares), lies between Mahajanga and Morondava and has an almost inaccessible maze of limestone needles and canyons as well as remote tombs of the Vazimba people, reputedly the country's earliest inhabitants. Toliara, in the southwest, is a fishing port and sisal-processing center. Crops such as peanuts, rice, and cotton are grown there.

Sunset lights the horizon behind a jagged landscape in the Tsingy de Bemaraha Nature Reserve in northwest Madagascar.

CLIMATE

Madagascar's climate is mostly tropical. The prevailing trade winds bring rain from the southeast, while monsoon winds blow from the northwest, resulting in more rain in the north than in the south. Rainfall varies from torrential storms on the east coast during February and March to dry conditions on the southwest, which may receive only 14 inches (36 centimeters) of rain a year. In general, the summer months from November to April are the wettest, with northwest air currents bringing the rain. Average summer temperatures range

A tenrec, one of Madagascar's unique mammals.

from 77 degrees Fahrenheit (25° Celsius) around the capital to 84°F (29°C) on the coast. Temperatures on the central highlands can drop to freezing during winter nights from June to August.

WILDLIFE

Madagascar's unique plants and animals are major tourist attractions. Approximately twelve thousand plants have been identified, representing about a third of the plants found in Africa. Madagascar not only has a record number of species unique to the island, but because of the continuing loss of forest cover, it also has one of the most threatened ecosystems in the world, plus more endangered species than any other country in Africa. For the Malagasy, rice cultivation and cattle raising are two of their most vital economic activities, and these cannot be carried out in a forest. As a result, trees have been cut down steadily for hundreds of years, so only about 20 percent of the original forests remain. Madagascar lost about 30 million acres (12 million ha) of forest between 1960 and 2000.

There are now sixty protected areas (nature reserves and national parks) maintained in partnership with the World Wildlife Fund, and traditional healers work with a team of Malagasy students to catalog the wealth of medicinal plants in the northern forests. The rosy periwinkle, for example, provides an essential compound used to treat childhood leukemia. Overseas agencies, such as the United States Agency for International Development (USAID) and the United Nations Educational, Scientific and Cultural Organization (UNESCO), also help to fund ecological preservation.

Among Madagascar's most famous mammals are the lemurs, which have apparently undergone little evolutionary change since the Eocene period about 50 million years ago. Another unusual animal is the tenrec, which looks like a tiny hedgehog with yellow and black stripes and bristling spines that rattle when it is angry. Among the thirty-three species of tenrec, some are furry. The largest is the size of a rabbit and is considered a food delicacy. There are thirty-seven species of bats, including fruit bats that are also known as flying foxes. Among the mongooselike carnivores is the fossa, which can be as large and as vicious as a puma. A rabbit-size, giant jumping rat, not unlike a wallaby, also lives there.

In the reptile world, Madagascar claims to be home to half of the world's species of chameleons. A chameleon's eyes swivel independently, allowing it to look forward and backward at the same time. A Malagasy proverb advises, "Be like the chameleon—keep one eye on the past and one eye on the future." There are also fringed geckos, boa constrictors, several species of tortoises and marine turtles, and over three hundred butterflies and moths. Birds are harder to spot. Among the rarer birds is the Madagascar flufftail.

Madagascar is considered one of the richest floral kingdoms in the world, with estimates of the number of species exceeding twelve thousand. There are, for example, 170 species of palms and 1,000 species of orchids. Many of the orchids grow on trees, where they live in harmony with the tree, collecting water as it runs down the trunk.

INTERNET LINKS

http://www.bbc.co.uk/nature/collections/p00db3n8
The BBC video series, "David Attenborough's Madagascar," has information about a wide variety of Malagasy fauna and flora.

http://evolution.berkeley.edu/evolibrary/news/091001_madagascar
This site provides a good explanation of the geographical formation of Madagascar and the development of its unique species.

http://www.worldatlas.com/articles/what-unique-animals-live-in-madagascar.html
Photos and information about the endemic animals of Madagascar are found on this site, along with links to related topics.

HISTORY

Fishing dugouts in Anakao, in southern Madagascar, are much like the ones used by the ancient Malagasy.

2

MADAGASCAR WAS ONE OF THE last places on earth to be occupied by human settlers. Before people arrived, the island's wildlife evolved over millennia of isolation, leading to the development of its many unique species. The first people arrived by way of outrigger canoes about two thousand years ago—not from Africa in the west as one might have guessed, but from the Sunda Islands of Indonesia some 4,000 miles (6,436 km) to the east.

Little is known about how or why they came. Some historians think the earliest settlers might have sailed straight across the Indian Ocean to Madagascar. Others believe the process took longer, with explorers making their way through India, Arabia, and Africa, intermarrying with local groups and acquiring their ethnic mix along the way. Known in local legend as the *Ntaolo* ("first men"), these "canoe people" are considered the ancestral guardians of the land.

Beginning in the seventh century, when Sumatra controlled trade in the Indian Ocean, more settlers, including Muslim traders, arrived. Different ethnic groups began to stake out various areas of the island to control as their own.

Since gaining independence from France in 1960, Madagascar has experienced repeated political instability. The nation has suffered coups, military dictatorship, assassinations, violent unrest, crippling general strikes, disputed elections, and political deadlock.

When the rich hauls of the West Indies pirates began to dwindle, the buccaneers of the sea diverted their attention to the trade routes around the Cape of Good Hope, India, and the East Indies. The east coast of Madagascar was an ideal base, and Nosy Boraha became their "home port." The island is a thin strip of land with coconut-fringed beaches surrounded by shallow seas. Captain William Kidd, an English buccaneer, arrived aboard his first ship, the Adventure, *in 1695, starting a life of piracy that ended on the gallows in London. Other infamous names include another English pirate, John Avery, the American pirate Thomas Tew, and the Frenchman Olivier Levasseur, also known as La Buse, meaning "The Buzzard," or possibly "The Fool." The names on the tombstones in the pirate graveyard in Nosy Boraha have long since worn away, but one skull and crossbones emblem can still be seen.*

EUROPEAN ARRIVALS

In 1500, Portuguese sailors were the first Europeans to arrive. They named their discovery the Isle of Saint Lawrence, but did not stay any longer than did later arrivals, the Dutch and the English. None of them thought the island was worth colonizing. The French did establish a colony in 1642, but plagued with disease and constant attacks by the local inhabitants, they packed up and left. More permanent residents were the bands of pirates operating in the area, especially along the eastern shore, washed by the immense Indian Ocean.

In the west, the Menabe peoples, with the help of firearms bought from European traders, extended their rule into the highlands as far as Bengy on the Sakalava River. Sakalava became the name of the people in that region. King Andriamisara I of the Menabe and his successor, Andriandahifotsy, came close to uniting southern and eastern Madagascar. Their successors ruled until the early nineteenth century, nearly two hundred years.

Robert Drury, a British sailor shipwrecked on Madagascar in 1703, stayed for sixteen years as a slave, royal butcher, and refugee. His journal is regarded as a historical source, although some commentators suspect that it was actually ghostwritten by Daniel Defoe, who padded Drury's story with descriptions written in 1658 by Etienne de Flacourt (a French governor of Madagascar) and added some reflections of his own. Defoe is the well-known author of *Robinson Crusoe*.

On the east coast, the pirate hotbed on Nosy Boraha attracted buccaneers from far away, and a forty-gun fort was built there to protect pirated goods. Around 1716, Ratsimilaho, the son of an English pirate and a Malagasy princess, united many of the rival coastal clans into the empire of Betsimisaraka, which means "those who stand together."

In 1750, his daughter Bety married a shipwrecked French corporal, and Ratsimilaho gave them the island of Nosy Boraha as a wedding gift. Upon Ratsimilaho's death, Princess Bety ruled in her father's place and ceded the island to France. Her son, who ruled after her, was unable to control local uprisings, and the Betsimisaraka kingdom shrank, becoming a single port.

THE MERINA KINGDOMS

In the meantime, the Merina people, led by King Andrianampoinimerina and his successor, Radama, were steadily increasing their domination of the central highlands by using weapons gained through trade agreements with European powers. In 1810 King Radama I modernized the army and, with thirty-five thousand men, established the largest kingdom yet in Madagascar. Unable to defeat the Sakalava kingdom of Menabe, Radama I arranged a marriage between his daughter and the Menabe king Ramitraho. Radama established positive relations with European powers, as well. A Frenchman was the general of his army and an Englishman, his adviser.

The capital was moved to Antananarivo by 1800, and the lucrative slave trade was stopped. In 1820 Britain signed a treaty recognizing Madagascar as an independent state under Merina rule. The London Missionary Society sent

Radama II, shown here in 1861, opened the country to Western influence in hopes of obtaining foreign money and modernizing ideas. But those new ideas alienated his supporters, and he was assassinated in 1863.

missionaries and converted the Merina court to Christianity. The missionaries taught skills to the people so that they could become blacksmiths, carpenters, printers, or weavers. The British also devised a Latin alphabet for the Merina dialect of Malagasy and set up a printing press. As a result, Merina culture began to spread over all of Madagascar.

In the late 1830s, King Radama's widow and successor, Queen Ranavalona I, declared Christianity illegal and killed many converts. Four churches in the capital city now stand in memory of those early martyrs. Her son, Radama II, ascended the throne in 1861 and established religious freedom. He improved the judicial system and encouraged foreign trade. Christianity became more or less official in Madagascar. Radama II was assassinated, however, after only two years on the throne.

A FRENCH COLONY

Competing European powers played a key role in the next chapter of Madagascar's history. In 1890 France and Britain signed a treaty in which French control over Madagascar was recognized in return for British sovereignty in Zanzibar. The French selected Mahajanga on the northwest coast of Madagascar as the base for their expeditionary force, which marched to Antananarivo in the central highlands.

By the time they arrived in the capital on September 30, 1895, the invading French force had shrunk to four thousand men—more than eleven thousand had died of disease along the way. But since sickness and starvation had also struck and weakened the Merina forces, the French still managed to capture the capital. In 1896 they set up a colonial administration with Joseph Galliéni as governor-general. In 1897 the French exiled the reigning Merina queen and turned Madagascar into a French protectorate.

Galliéni proclaimed French the official language and tried to suppress both the Malagasy language and the earlier British influence. The colonial settlers cleared the forests to make way for sugarcane, cotton, and coffee plantations. Harsh taxation resulted in forced labor for those unable to pay, and many peasants were compelled to work in conditions of semislavery. Although the island was developed under French rule, and there were construction projects and visible economic progress, among the people there were increasing resentments and an accelerating desire for national independence.

During the early stages of World War II, France fell to Germany. British forces then occupied several major towns on the island, including Antananarivo and the port of Diégo-Suarez, to prevent the harbor from falling into Japanese hands, allies of Germany. Madagascar was handed back to the French, led by General Charles de Gaulle, in 1943, and became an Overseas Territory of France (an administrative division of France outside of Europe) in 1946. In the highland plateau, though, the smoldering struggle for political rights by the Merina led to an uprising in March 1947 that was crushed ruthlessly by the French army. Several thousand Malagasy were killed, and the leaders were either executed or exiled. Seeing the way the political winds were blowing, however, the French then began to let go and transfer political power to the leaders of the coastal regions.

Philibert Tsiranana was Madagascar's first president.

In 1958 the Malagasy people voted in a referendum to become an autonomous republic within the French community of overseas nations. Independence was at last achieved on June 26, 1960 (now celebrated as Independence Day), and Philibert Tsiranana was elected as the first president of the Malagasy Republic.

THE FIRST REPUBLIC

The recent history of Madagascar has been greatly influenced by the struggles for power between two main ethnic groups: the *côtiers* (COH-ti-ay), or coastal people, and the highland Merina. Although supposedly independent, Madagascar continued to be dominated by France, which remained in control of trade and financial institutions. President Tsiranana was pro-French and refused to establish diplomatic relations with Communist countries. The

President Didier Ratsiraka in 1975

Merina disliked him because he was a *côtier*. The economy fell into a slump, and uprisings were suppressed as harshly as they had been under French rule.

Massive antigovernment demonstrations took place in 1972, forcing President Tsiranana to resign. The civilian government was replaced by a military one when General Gabriel Ramanantsoa was appointed prime minister. A period of martial law followed during which a new leader, Colonel Richard Ratsimandrava, was shot dead within a week of taking office. In June 1975, the Supreme Council of the Revolution, led by Admiral Didier Ratsiraka, ushered in a Christian-Marxist one-party state, changing the name of the country from the Malagasy Republic to the Democratic Republic of Madagascar.

THE SECOND REPUBLIC

President Ratsiraka found himself at the helm of a country with a shattered economy and a nonexistent educational system. He nationalized banks, insurance companies, and major businesses. He cut ties with France, and welcomed military help from the Soviet Union. A debt crisis in 1981, however, forced Ratsiraka to rethink these reforms and he returned to a free market economy in 1986.

In 1982 he was reelected to a second seven-year term, but mounting unrest forced him to allow opposition parties to be introduced during the run-up to the 1989 elections. In spite of this, he was elected to a third term as president. Widespread allegations of ballot rigging abounded, and a string of protest riots erupted. Amid the fall of communism in Eastern Europe and the crumbling of the Soviet Union, Ratsiraka maintained friendly relations with North Korea and made trade agreements with the apartheid government of South Africa.

The main opposition, the Forces Vives, called for general strikes. Nearly half a million people staged demonstrations in front of the presidential palace, demanding democracy. The presidential guard opened fire on the demonstrators and many were killed. In November 1991, President Ratsiraka relinquished power, but refused to step down from his official position.

A transitional government formed to draft a new constitution, which was approved by referendum in August 1992. This declared Madagascar to be a unitary state with multiparty democracy and reduced the executive powers of the president. In the subsequent presidential elections, Albert Zafy, a French-trained professor of surgery and leader of the Forces Vives, was elected, ending seventeen years of Ratsiraka's virtual dictatorship. Zafy became the first president of the Third Republic in March 1993.

THE THIRD REPUBLIC

The Third Republic was not immune to problems. President Zafy was soon impeached, in 1996, for corruption and unconstitutional exercise of power. Zafy's government was also ineffective in implementing International Monetary Fund (IMF) policies to modernize and promote Madagascar's economy. The increasingly distressed population held public demonstrations and called for a military government in response to the worsening economic situation. In the ensuing presidential elections of 1997, former president Ratsiraka emerged the winner. A 1998 referendum returned more power to the presidency, making impeachment more difficult and allowing the president to dissolve parliament.

The next round of presidential elections in 2001 led to political disaster when Ratsiraka's main opponent, Marc Ravalomanana, contested the electoral results on the grounds that Ratsiraka had rigged the election. A six-month political crisis ensued, and Madagascar's economy virtually came to a standstill as violence broke out among rival protesters. The charismatic Ravalomanana was eventually declared president in May 2002. He began implementing economic reforms that won the support of donors and investors from the West. Although poverty remained widespread, Ravalomanana did manage to return the economy to pre-conflict levels and to retire foreign debt.

Before the 2006 elections, barred presidential hopeful General Fidy Andrianafidisoa attempted to stage a military coup to derail Ravalomanana's electoral campaign. The coup failed to materialize, and he was later arrested. Ravalomanana managed to secure a second five-year term in December 2006.

POLITICAL CRISIS

Political strife continued, however, and the president became involved in a power struggle with the mayor of Antananarivo, Andry Rajoelina. In January 2009, Rajoelina organized protests against the president's increasingly authoritarian policies, which then turned violent, deadly, and destructive. The rallies and violence went on for weeks. In February, guards at the Ambohitsorohitra Palace in the capital city opened fire on demonstrators, killing and injuring scores of people. The killings revived the opposition, which had been waning up to that point. Rajoelina, meanwhile, announced the creation of an alternative, transitional government and his supporters took over government ministries. Tensions escalated, attempts at peace talks failed, and the military became involved. Analysts feared a civil war would break out between the supporters of both sides. In March, President Ravalomanana resigned, handing power over to the military, and fleeing the country. Ravalomanana would later state, "I never resigned. I was forced to hand power over, at gun point, on March the seventeenth."

The military handed power over to Rajoelina, who was called the President of the High Authority of Transition (HTA) of Madagascar. For the most part, the international community condemned the power transfer as a *coup d'*état, the illegal overthrow of an existing government. Various nations instituted sanctions on Madagascar, including the United States, which suspended all non-humanitarian assistance.

In the end, the violence associated with the political crisis resulted in a death toll of at least 130. Madagascar remained diplomatically isolated and cut off from much needed donor aid and tourism revenue. The setback to the country's economy was enormous, and it deeply impacted the lives of the Malagasy people in ways from which they are still trying to recover.

In 2010, voters in Madagascar approved a new constitution, which launched the country's Fourth Republic. The change was widely regarded as an attempt to consolidate and legitimize Rajoelina's HTA government. The new constitution lowered the minimum age for presidential candidates from forty to thirty-five. This made Rajoelina, aged thirty-six at the time, eligible to run in the next presidential election.

THE FOURTH REPUBLIC

In January 2013, an agreement brokered by the South African Development Community (SADC) stipulated that neither Rajoelina nor Ravalomanana would run in the upcoming presidential election, which would take place within six months. The two bitter rivals agreed, but then put up their respective wives for election. The country's electoral court intervened and put a stop to those shenanigans.

An election of bona fide candidates finally took place in October 2013, ultimately naming Hery Martial Rakotoarimanana Rajaonarimampianina as the new president. He took office in January 2014. The following year, after some further shifting of political loyalties, Malagasy lawmakers in the National Assembly voted in favor of impeaching Rajaonarimampianina. However, the country's High Constitutional Court ruled against it, stating that the request was unfounded.

President Hery Rajaonarimampianina addresses delegates at the India-Africa Summit in New Delhi, India, in October 2015.

INTERNET LINKS

http://www.bbc.com/news/world-africa-13864364
This BBC News timeline highlights key events in Malagasy history.

https://www.britannica.com/place/Madagascar/History
This online encyclopedia offers an in-depth history of the island.

http://www.lonelyplanet.com/madagascar/history
A quick overview of Malagasy history is provided on this travel site.

GOVERNMENT

Peaceful demonstrators gather around the Malagasy flag.

MADAGASCAR IS A REPUBLIC WITH a semi-presidential form of government. A republic is a representative democracy in which the people's elected representatives, not the people themselves, vote on legislation. A presidential system is one in which the executive branch exists separately from the legislature. A semi-presidential government is one in which the president shares power with a prime minister and a cabinet. Together, the president and the prime minister are responsible to the legislature.

From its earliest history up to 1975, Madagascar was subject to many kinds of governments—the rule of independent kingdoms, such as the Merina and Menabe; the control by a European colonial power (1897—1958); the autocratic wielding of power by President Philibert Tsiranana (1959—1972), followed by the introduction of a Marxist one-party state during the first term of President Didier Ratsiraka (1976—1993).

The political theory of Marxism holds that, ideally, a country progresses from allegiance to a local ruler (feudalism) to privately owned production (capitalism) to public ownership of a country's assets (socialism) to the eventual goal of a classless society (communism).

In Madagascar, however, communism brought economic ruin. Although President Ratsiraka instituted some private sector reforms in the late 1980s in a bid to curb government debt, growing dissatisfaction persisted among the public with the country's political and economic conditions. This eventually led, in 1992, to a new constitution, the creation of a multiparty political system, and reduced executive powers for the president. Economic decline continued, however, and the unhappy public called for a military government in early 1996. Ratsiraka's successor, President Albert Zafy, was impeached, allowing Ratsiraka to pull off a comeback in the election of February 1997. He then won a referendum to expand presidential power. In the 2001 presidential election, Ratsiraka was overthrown by Marc Ravalomanana. Under President Ravalomanana, Madagascar became a democratic republic with a free market economy.

THE CONSTITUTION

Annexed by France as a colony in 1896, the Malagasy Republic, as it was then called, became self-governing in 1958. The island gained full independence in 1960 and changed its name to the Democratic Republic of Madagascar in 1975. Ruled by President Didier Ratsiraka as La Deuxième République, meaning the Second Republic, from 1975 to 1992, Madagascar tried to adopt Marxism, nationalizing foreign banks and firms.

Under the 1975 constitution, there was a People's National Assembly, with 137 members elected by the people. Nevertheless, a twenty-two-member Supreme Revolutionary Council, two-thirds of whom were appointed by the president, made the most important decisions. For practical matters of administration, the president appointed a Council of Ministers that was headed by the prime minister. Those seventeen years are now regarded as a dictatorship.

A new constitution, ratified in August 1992, ushered in the Third Republic. It introduced a more democratic government and several political parties were formed. In 1998 the constitution was amended to strengthen the presidency. Changes included the expansion of presidential power to handpick one-third of the senators and the removal of the legislature's control over the prime minister and cabinet. More revisions were made to the constitution in April 2007, including the creation of twenty-two smaller regions to replace the six autonomous regions and the enlargement of presidential powers in cases of emergency.

Madagascar's current constitution dates from December 2010, which marked the transition to the Fourth Republic. The new constitution lowered the minimum age for presidential candidates from forty to thirty-five. This made thirty-six-year-old Andry Rajoelina, the head of the High Transitional Authority (HAT) government that had overthrown Ravalomanana, eligible to run for president in the next election. In the end, however, he did not run.

Newly appointed Madagascar Prime Minister Olivier Mahafaly Solonandrasana delivers a speech during the swearing-in ceremony at Mazoharivo Palace on April 13, 2016 in Antananarivo.

EXECUTIVE BRANCH

The president is the head of state and the prime minister is the head of government. The president holds executive power. As of 2017, the president is Hery Rajaonarimampianina (b. 1958); and the prime minister is Olivier Mahafaly Solonandrasana (b. 1964).

The president is elected by the vote of the people for a term of five years, while the prime minister is nominated by the National Assembly and appointed by the president. He handles the day-to-day running of the country together with the Council of Ministers. The president also has the power to dissolve the National Assembly, the lower chamber of the Madagascan parliament.

As the *ray aman-dreny* (ray AH-mahn-dray-n), a traditional title previously reserved for the king, the president is to ensure respect for the constitution and be responsible for national sovereignty and integrity. The person of the president is also the symbol of national unity.

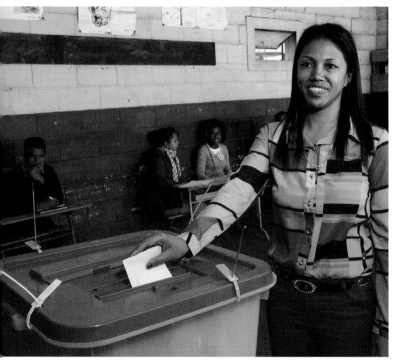

LEGISLATIVE BRANCH

The parliament is bicameral, consisting of the National Assembly and the Senate. Both have the power to create legislation and the next election for both houses will be in December 2021.

ANTENIMIERAN-DOHOLONA (SENATE) The Senate has sixty-three members, forty-two of whom are elected by local legislators, with the remainder appointed by the president. The Senate was dissolved following the 2009 coup and was reestablished in December 2015. Members serve six-year terms.

Lalatiana Rakotondrazafy, a candidate for a local-level office, casts her ballot at a polling station in Antananarivo during municipal elections in 2015.

ANTENIMIERAMPIRENENA (NATIONAL ASSEMBLY) The National Assembly, which consists of 151 members, serve under the prime minister. Eighty-seven members are directly elected in single-seat constituencies by a simple majority vote and sixty-four are directly elected in multi-seat constituencies by a closed-list proportional representation vote. Members serve four-year terms. The next election will be in December 2021.

JUDICIAL BRANCH

The judicial system is modeled after that of France. It includes the Supreme Court in Antananarivo, the High Constitutional Court, and the Court of Appeal. There are eleven courts of first instance for civil and commercial cases, and ordinary criminal courts in most towns for criminal cases. Most judges and magistrates have had French training, but the traditional law of the Merina and other ethnic groups is taken into account by state magistrates when judging marriage, family, land, and inheritance cases.

NATIONAL DEFENSE

Since 1975, Madagascar's army, navy, air force, and police have been incorporated into one body, the People's Armed Forces—consisting of the army, 12,500-strong; navy, 500, including 100 marines; air force, 500; and the National Gendarmerie, a military body charged with police duties that is 8,100-strong. Madagascar has no need for a large military force, so its small army is used mainly for maintaining law and order in conjunction with the gendarmes. However, it did become involved in the civil strife and political overthrow of the government in 2009.

Officially, there is compulsory military service of eighteen months for males ages eighteen to twenty-five, but not all conscripts are called up. Women are not drafted but can volunteer for all services except the Navy. The term of service obligation is eighteen months for the military or the equivalent in civil service. The National Gendarmerie recruits men between twenty and thirty years of age, or up to thirty-five years for those with military experience.

Soldiers guard the prime minister's office during the civil strife in 2009 as the High Transitional Authority (HAT) government grabbed power.

Both police and army personnel wear camouflage khaki uniforms and can be difficult to distinguish from one another. The police usually wear a blue kepi, a cap with a flat circular top and a visor that used to be worn in the French military, while soldiers often have red or black berets.

INTERNET LINKS

http://www.bbc.com/news/world-africa-13861843
The BBC News provides a profile of the country and its president.

https://www.cia.gov/library/publications/the-world-factbook/geos/ma.html
The CIA World Factbook has up-to-date information on the government of Madagascar.

ECONOMY

A Malagasy worker bundles vanilla beans in Antalaha.

4

LIKE MANY AFRICAN NATIONS, Madagascar is a very poor country. Indeed, with an extreme poverty rate of over 70 percent in 2012, Madagascar is among the poorest of the poor. And like the other former European colonies in Africa, it has had a difficult time building a strong, stable economy since winning independence half a century ago.

Despite its many potential natural resources, the island nation faces enormous economic challenges. It made some progress in the early 2000s, with the help of World Bank and International Monetary Fund (IMF) initiatives, but a political crisis from 2009 to 2013 destroyed most of that momentum. Today, the country's efforts at improvement are compromised by political instability, rampant government corruption, a weak judicial system, and serious environmental problems. Madagascar is also one of the ten countries most at risk from the effects of global warming.

However, there are signs of progress once again. Following the democratic election of a new president in 2014, the IMF approved a Rapid Credit Facility (quick financial assistance in the form of a zero-interest loan) to Madagascar worth about $42.1 million to help the government meet its balance of payments needs. In mid-2016, based on the country's satisfactory performance, the IMF approved another $304 million loan. Additional support has been provided by the African Development Bank, the World Bank, and the United Nations Development Programme

After saffron, vanilla is the second most expensive spice in the world. During the colonial period, Madagascar vanilla growers began branding their beans with unique designs to help identify them in cases of theft. The tiny marks are engraved on the bean two weeks before harvest, and remain visible even after the curing and drying processes.

(UBDP)—as well as by private donors. The economy has shown growth of about 2.6 percent a year in recent years and is expected to continue at that rate, and possibly even better.

ECONOMIC HISTORY

Before 1972, following the French colonial style, the government established producers' cooperatives that collected and processed most of the rice harvested in the country. The farmers were paid extremely low prices that they resented bitterly. The disquiet over this important crop led to domestic turbulence and a shift in economic policy.

The post-1975 military regime attempted to introduce a "socialist paradise," and formerly French-dominated firms were nationalized. The government also created state monopolies for import-export trading, and the textile, cotton, and power industries became regulated. In spite of these resolute measures, the economy declined, and the poorest people were hit the hardest. The rural population struggled to survive day by day, bartering with cattle and bags of coarse rice. By 1982 Madagascar was technically bankrupt.

In June 1990, France wrote off Madagascar's debt of 4 billion French francs in response to moves by President Didier Ratsiraka to accept a free-market economy, which included disbanding agricultural marketing boards and diversifying traditional primary exports. The economy did not revive straightaway, but from 1997 to 2001 solid economic growth was seen, with foreign investments, further privatizations, and the development of an export processing zone (EPZ) where tariffs and quotas were eliminated, contributing to the slow-growing success.

This success was derailed by the six-month political crisis over the disputed outcome of the presidential elections in December 2001. Economic activity came to a halt when Ratsiraka's forces blockaded the capital,

A woman works in a rice field.

Vanilla is said to be the world's most popular flavor—in fact, vanilla is essential in the making of chocolate! But keeping the world supplied with this beloved ingredient isn't easy. It begins with a flower. The flat-leaved vanilla orchid, the plant that produces the vanilla bean, is surprisingly finicky. It grows only in very limited climatic zones in the tropics—in Madagascar, it's grown mostly on the hot, wet east coast. Each single flower opens for only one day a year; and if it isn't pollinated, it doesn't produce a bean.

Leaving the matter to nature is too uncertain, depending as it does on only one genus of bee found in Mexico, where the vanilla orchid originated. Therefore, vanilla farmers must hand pollinate the flowers, one by one. It's a sensitive process which, if successful, results nine months later in seedpods about 6 to 8 inches (15 to 20 cm) long. These are picked, blanched in vats of boiling water, and then dried in the sun for about five months. Growing vanilla is extremely labor intensive.

Madagascar vanilla is among the best in the world. Together with Réunion and the Comoros islands, Madagascar is a leading producer of the bean. In 2015, Indonesia took the top spot in world vanilla production, with 3,200 tons (2,903 metric tons), just barely exceeding Madagascar's 3,100 tons (2,812 t). Production in other vanilla-growing nations, including third-place Mexico, falls far behind.

Today, Madagascar provides about half of the world's supply of vanilla, and most of its crop goes to the United States. There it is used by the ice cream industry and in the making of cola drinks (in which vanilla is an essential ingredient). In recent years there has been a boom in vanilla prices. In the 1990s, vanilla sold for roughly $9 a pound ($4.08/kilogram), but with climate change, widespread drought, and increased demand, prices have risen steadily. In 2015, that price climbed to $220/lb ($100/kg) and in 2017, following a cyclone in Madagascar which damaged 30 percent of the crop, vanilla beans reached a record high of over $1,300/lb ($600/kg). Despite those astonishing prices, the Malagasy vanilla farmers are typically very poor and live a hard life. Rising prices have led to vanilla-related thefts, murders, and poaching.

difficult to breed them for meat consumption or export. Other domestic animals are sheep, goats, pigs, chickens, geese, and turkeys. The Malagasy consider their wild animals, such as the lemurs, of little importance, although they are beginning to realize that tourists who show an interest in the creatures are a source of revenue.

Although fishing has been relatively slow to develop as an industry, fish products in recent years have become significant sources of export revenue. Madagascar allows four joint-venture companies and vessels from the European Union to conduct commercial fishing in exchange for compensation. French investment has also helped establish a tuna cannery. Inland, irrigated rice fields are stocked with breeding fish, although the catch is used mainly for local consumption. Tourist hotels offer good quality seafood that includes tuna, plaice (flounder), lobster, crab, calamari (squid), and prawns.

Fishermen in Maroantsetra empty a netful of fish caught using traditional methods in 2016.

FORESTRY

Forests cover 21.5 percent of the land surface and contain many valuable hardwoods, such as ebony, rosewood, and sandalwood. Gums, resins, and plants used in tanning and dyeing and for medicinal purposes are found in many wooded places. Farming people need open land to cultivate rice and to pasture their goats and cattle, however, so they cut down the trees unsparingly.

The timber is used to supply 82 percent of household fuel, either in the form of logs or as charcoal, and as a result, the amount of forested land shrinks alarmingly every year. Most of the wood and charcoal used for fuel is illegally obtained, taken from supposedly protected areas. This ceaseless deforestation allows the valuable topsoil to be washed away.

Although there are many narrow valleys with fast-flowing waterfalls, only a small number have been harnessed for hydroelectric power. Only 15 percent of the population has access to electricity—37 percent in urban areas and a mere 4 percent in rural areas. Thermal plants are another source of power. Bottled propane gas is often used for cooking.

TOURISM

Madagascar has much to offer tourists, and if the facilities and marketing were improved, the economy might enjoy immense benefits. But the islands of Mauritius and the Seychelles lure visitors away with their better hotels and transportation services. The real

A "dancing" lemur makes for an amusing sight for tourists in the Berenty Nature Reserve.

attractions of Madagascar are its unique flora and fauna and the friendliness of its people. Until roads, transportation services, and accommodations are improved, however, the majority of tourists will be hardy travelers prepared to rough it out.

Specially created reserves such as Périnet (east of Antananarivo) and Berenty or Kaleta Park (in the south) are proving to be beneficial to tourists and local residents alike. In the parks, wildlife can be viewed easily along walking trails where lemurs will tumble out of the trees at the wave of a banana. They stand momentarily upright and then dance sideways, tail looped high, looking perpetually surprised. The parks also provide employment for wardens, guides, and maintenance staff.

Trees and rare wildlife are being preserved—provided thieves do not gain access first. There are also ecological tourism centers that offer audiovisual explanations of the areas, like the one at Andohahela near Tôlanaro. The islands of Nosy Be and Nosy Boraha are sprucing up, too, and are becoming increasingly popular with overseas visitors for the scuba diving and snorkeling that showcase some of the most beautiful coral reefs in the region. Nosy Boraha also provides whale-watching tours, as migrating humpback whales gather off the island to breed from July to September.

COMMUNICATION

No one will deny that the island's road transportation system is in a poor state. Only some 16 percent of the roads are paved, and most of those are full of potholes. The other roads are dirt trails that are often impassable in the wet season. In theory, the Malagasy drive on the right-hand side of the road, but in fact they drive wherever there are any visible fragments of hard surface. They drive their vehicles (most of them French)

A rickshaw bicycle driver looks for customers in the city of Toamasina.

very carefully, partly out of courtesy to other motorists but mainly because replacement parts are almost impossible to find. Most people travel by oxcart or *taxi-brousse* (TAK-see-BROOSS), a minibus or pickup truck.

Flying is the favored way to travel for those who can afford it, and the Malagasy wear their best clothes for their trips: ladies in fine dresses and men in smart shirts. The national airline was originally called Mad Air, until somebody thought it disrespectful. They renamed it Air Madagascar, so now it is known as Air Mad. Air France, Air Mauritius, and France's Corsair fly in from abroad. There is an international airport at Antananarivo and twenty-five other airfields with paved runways in most major towns around the island.

Much of the transportation system serves Antananarivo, and carriers travel only to the slightly richer areas of the high plateau and the ports on the east coast. There are only two railway lines that connect the plateau with the east coast: one links Fianarantsoa to the port of Manakara, and the other runs from Antananarivo to Toamasina. Each seldom runs more than one train a day. The line from Antananarivo to Toamasina is 235 miles (378 km) long. Built between 1901 and 1913, it is both a scenic wonder and a considerable engineering feat. To improve Madagascar's rail system, the government granted Mandarail a twenty-five-year concession to operate the national railroad. Operations began in 2003. The Pangalanes Canal offers a waterway of lagoons linked by canals along the east coast, but it is poorly maintained and only isolated stretches are usable.

The poor infrastructure prevents the postal system from being very reliable. Cell phones, however, are fairly well served by three mobile service providers for the 47 percent of the people who use phones. Madagascar has six Internet service providers for its 994,000 users.

THE FUTURE

Madagascar's economic survival seems to depend on preserving and improving its natural environment—one of its strongest potential resources—and finding a way to capitalize on its other resources, such as minerals and oil. Widespread poverty is both a huge motivation for improving the economy and a huge obstacle as well. Strategic alliances with NGOs, private investors, and international financial institutions are helping to reduce poverty, but for these to succeed will require political and domestic stability.

INTERNET LINKS

http://www.aljazeera.com/indepth/features/2017/01/bitter-taste-madagascar-vanilla-170131073036652.html
This article examines the hard life of a Malagasy vanilla farmer.

https://www.export.gov/article?id=Madagascar-Market-Overview
This site provides an up-to-date report on Madagascar's economic situation.

ENVIRONMENT

This panther chameleon is one of Madagascar's endemic animals.

5

MADAGASCAR REMAINED untouched by human hands for longer than most places on earth. Today, however, the human influence is all too evident in the deforestation of the island. This has led to the country's most devastating environmental problems.

Madagascar is renowned for its beauty and tremendous biodiversity. More than two hundred thousand known species of flora and fauna have made the island their home, living in habitats ranging from the rugged mountains in the north to the spiny desert in the south and to the lush rain forests, rolling hills, and mangrove swamps in between. Some 150,000 of these species are not found anywhere else on the planet. Regrettably, the arrival of humans led to the long and unrelenting process of degradation and extinction of the island's wondrous plant and animal life.

DEFORESTATION

In Madagascar, 80 percent of the people are dependent on the island's natural resources for sustenance. The island's economy is largely based on agriculture. Traditionally, the people have cleared away forest to grow rice and cassava, to keep up charcoal production, and to burn bushes to maintain pastureland for grazing their goats and prized zebu cattle. Every year as much as a third of Madagascar's remaining forest is burned to sustain these practices.

Many thousands of Madagascar's plant and animal species grow nowhere else on the earth—and scientists are continuing to discover more endemic species all the time. From 1999 to 2010, scientists discovered 615 new species in Madagascar, including forty-one mammals and sixty-one reptiles.

Slash-and-burn farming in Madagascar, a practice locally called "tavy," is normally practiced to convert tropical rain forests to rice fields. Usually an acre or two (0.4 or 0.8 ha) of forest is cut, burned, and later planted with rice. Such techniques can yield rice production for about two years before the field must be left to lie fallow (dormant) for the next four to six years. Rice is then cultivated again for two or three more cycles. By the third cycle, the soil is usually too stripped of essential nutrients to support further rice farming. Scrub vegetation and wild grasses then overrun the tired soil. Soil erosion becomes a problem, especially during heavy rains, because, unlike trees, these alien vegetations cannot anchor the soil well.

Madagascar loses so much soil to erosion that its rivers run blood red, causing huge stains in the surrounding Indian Ocean. About 80 percent of the country's original vegetation has already been destroyed, and today much of the country is sterile grassland, with arable land making up only 5 percent of the total land area.

The denuded landscape of deforestation in Madagascar.

Slash and burn is a method of agriculture used in the tropics, typically by subsistence farmers, to clear land for cultivation. Forest vegetation is cut down and burned, and the land is planted with crops or used for grazing cattle. After a few years, the soil is

exhausted and the farmers move on to new land and repeat the process. Meanwhile, on the previously cleared land, new vegetation takes over.

Slash and burn is one of the oldest methods of farming, dating from prehistoric times. However, in today's world of limited land and depleted forests, this form of agriculture contributes to a number of ecological problems.

Deforestation—When large numbers of people clear forest faster than it can recover, a permanent loss of forest cover may result.

Nutrient Loss—When large swaths of land are slashed, burned, and cultivated in rapid succession, nutrients are used up or leached from the soil, leaving it permanently unable to sustain vegetation of any sort.

Erosion—Without root systems holding soil in place, the soil is easily displaced by wind, weather, and gravity.

Desertification—Nutrient loss and erosion lead to desertification, a situation in which previously fertile land turns into desert. The dry, barren soil is infertile and unable to support growth of any kind. The added pressures of climate change speed up this process.

Biodiversity Loss—When plots of land are cleared, the various plants and animals that lived in that habitat can no longer survive there. If a certain area is the only one supporting a particular species, slashing and burning can cause the extinction of that species. In tropical regions where biodiversity is extremely high, the danger of extinction may be magnified.

The golden-crowned sifaka is a rare species of lemur.

Soil erosion brings with it a host of other problems, most of which threaten the way of life of the people. Surrounding water becomes undrinkable as it is polluted with silt, fisheries suffer as fish roes are smothered with soil sediments, and floods become increasingly devastating as siltation raises the riverbeds. Transportation networks disintegrate because roads that cut across forests become dangerously impassable. The Malagasy people are not alone in suffering the effects of these agricultural practices—the island's plant and animal species are also affected.

ENDANGERED FLORA AND FAUNA

Madagascar has one of the richest and most unique assortment of flora and fauna in the world, and 85 percent of its flora and a majority of its fauna—39 percent of birds, 91 percent of reptiles, 99 percent of amphibians, and 100 percent of lemurs are endemic, native, to the country. It can therefore be considered an ecological catastrophe that so much of Madagascar's flora and fauna are being driven to the brink of extinction as a result of deforestation, forest fires, and overgrazing that can lead to desertification.

In 2007 the World Conservation Union listed 37 of Madagascar's major fauna as critically endangered, 88 as endangered, and 137 as vulnerable. This list includes 47 of the island's threatened mammalian species. The mammals include the golden-crowned sifaka lemur, the hairy-eared dwarf lemur, and the humpback whale. Some 35 bird species and 280 plant species are also endangered.

The lucrative worldwide market for endangered animal products, such as snake leather and tortoise shells, has led to the further decimation of animal habitats. The rare plowshare tortoise in northeast Madagascar can bring an estimated $30,000 on the black market. Looting and smuggling of such species for a quick cash gain poses a long-term danger of serious ecological imbalance.

CONSERVATION

The government has so far been ineffective at preserving the country's rich ecological heritage. In 2003 it pumped about $18 million into the protection and conservation of the environment, with plans to spend millions more. Foreign donors and other international organizations have been lending Madagascar a hand in the protection of its environment. The World Bank has helped to sponsor Madagascar's sixty protected areas, including nature reserves and national parks. The World Wildlife Fund (WWF) has partnered with Madagascar to carry out several ecological projects, as have numerous other nongovernmental organizations. However, Madagascar's 2009 political crisis threw the best of intentions off schedule for a few years.

Despite all that, slash—and—burn practices, erosion, and soil degradation continue to contribute to the degradation of the country's ecological stability. These factors, along with illegal logging, impede forest regrowth. Although some regions are seeing an increase in tree cover, this is largely due to non-native invasive species taking hold. Data from 2001—2012 suggests that, in general, the rate of forest loss in Madagascar has continued to increase.

The Malagasy themselves may understand that the island's natural environment is fragile and needs to be protected. But the practical need to feed their growing families is greater than the need for environmental conservation. For conservation to be successful, the government must reconcile the immediate needs of the people with the long-term benefits that conservation can yield. Good socioeconomic practices need to be implemented to generate a sustainable environment.

To decrease the dependence on charcoal, the government is also encouraging the use of biofuels such as palm oil, jatropha plants, soy, and sugarcane as alternative energy resources.

Rice cultivation is a deeply ingrained cultural practice that came over from South Asia with the very earliest settlers. New techniques of cultivation may take a while to catch on. One method of restoring degraded land is through using the permaculture system of developing efficient ecosystems by planting *savoka* (sah-VOOK) gardens consisting of a mixture of carefully

MADAGASCAR'S MEGAFAUNA

Before humans set foot on Madagascar around two thousand years ago, there lived on the island huge tortoises, giant predatory raptors (whose eggs were said to be big enough to make an omelet to feed 150 people), pygmy hippopotamuses, and enormous lemurs, the largest of which had the body mass of a male gorilla. These endemic animals were the biggest animals on the island— the megafauna. Explorations at cave, marsh, and stream sites have shown that competition with man for food, habitat, and space led to the gradual annihilation of the megafauna. Also found were subfossils of at least seventeen extinct species of lemurs. Sharp cuts and chop marks characteristic of skinning and filleting were found on lemur bones, evidence that humans ate them into extinction.

Although these titans no longer walk on earth, their remains nonetheless provide compelling examples of the staggering and distinctive biodiversity that make up Madagascar.

Two Malagasy men show off their discovery of an unbroken eggshell of the extinct Aepyornis, also called the elephant bird.

selected native forest plants and fruits or vegetable plants cultivated on fallow plots of land. These plants not only enrich the soil they also yield a steady stream of food crops. Ginger, for example, adds phosphorus to the soil, while leguminous plants (peas and beans) reintroduce lost nitrogen. Other plants such as vanilla, banana, coffee, and rubber also help to restore lost nutrients. Such sustainable use of soil can help in maintaining biological diversity and the preservation of Madagascar's forests for decades.

Ecotourism and teaching about the environment in schools are other moves to encourage and raise national awareness of environmental conservation practices.

ECOLOGICAL TREATIES

The preservation of the environment is an ongoing battle in Madagascar. As early as two hundred years ago, the Merina king Andrianampoinimerina recognized the need to protect the island's great trees. He punished those who deforested large swaths of land, but the practice continued. The island's efforts to protect its ecology legally began with the French in 1927. The colonial government established ten reserves to halt the ever-diminishing forest cover. This proved unsuccessful as well.

Effective conservation gained momentum only in the late 1980s when Madagascar worked with the WWF to evaluate all the protected areas in the country and to provide people living near the reserves with economically viable alternatives to many destructive customs.

Today Madagascar is party to a long list of international agreements and treaties relevant to conservation and climate change.

INTERNET LINKS

http://rainforests.mongabay.com/20madagascar.htm
This site uses maps and charts to illustrate Madagascar's environmental situation.

https://www.worldwildlife.org/places/madagascar
The WWF discusses some of Madagascar's most important environmental problems.

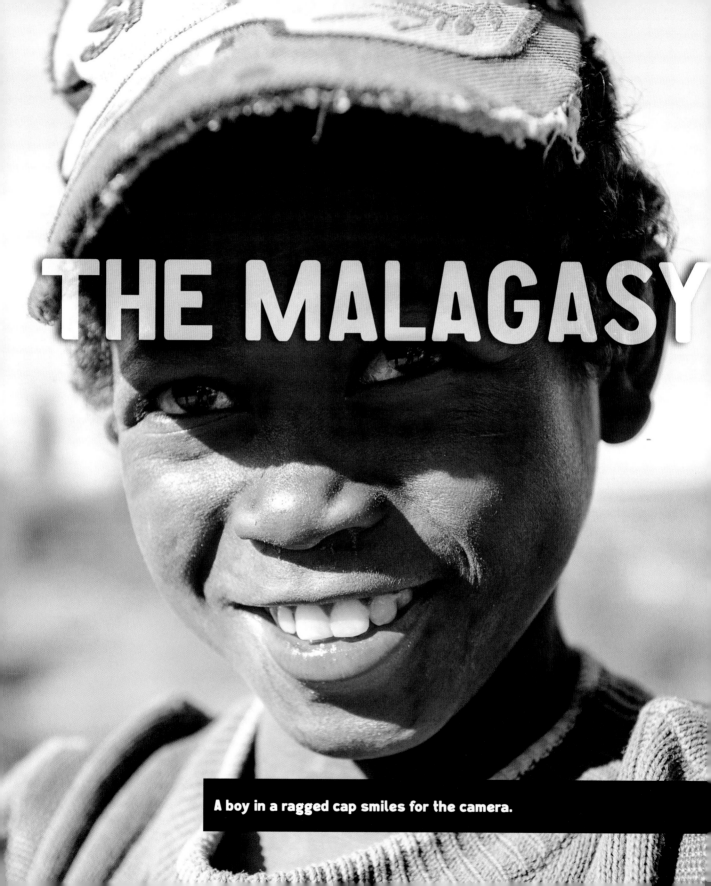

THE MALAGASY

A boy in a ragged cap smiles for the camera.

6

T HE PEOPLE OF MADAGASCAR ARE called the Malagasy. (In French the word is *Malgache*.) Although the country is geographically close to Africa and is included in most lists of African countries, most Malagasy do not consider themselves Africans. Those living in the Central Highlands are mostly short and slim. They have straight black hair, light brown skin, dark eyes, and high cheekbones, indicative of their Malay or Indonesian origins. Along the coast, people are often strikingly tall and much darker, with curly hair, indicating their descent from later African immigrants.

Determining demographic information about the Malagasy is difficult because most data is out of date and therefore must be estimated. The last population census took place in 1993, following an initial census in 1975. The government tried to administer a census in 2009, but was unsuccessful due to political instability. Therefore, current population figures are constructed from growth trends and compiled data from other sources—such as church memberships and school enrollments.

Vazaha is the word the Malagasy use to refer to non-Malagasy people. For the most part, the word is used in reference to white people, but it can also stand in for anything not of Malagasy origin. One can speak Vazaha, listen to Vazaha music, and so forth. As for the Malagasy themselves, they tend to go by the nickname *Gasys*.

ORIGINS

No one is certain how or when the original settlers arrived in Madagascar. No physical evidence of human habitation has been found dating earlier than about two thousand years ago. Most historians and anthropologists agree that the first inhabitants were Malayo-Polynesians who crossed the Indian Ocean from Indonesia and Southeast Asia two millennia ago. However, in academic circles, the subject of Malagasy origins remains an unsolved mystery, and new archaeological studies are examining genetic samples from today's population to try to solve that puzzle.

According to Malagasy culture, however, the first inhabitants of the island were the Vazimba, a pastoral clan that tended herds of zebu cattle on the central plateau long before the Merina arrived. Some versions of regional oral tradition say the Vazimba were a pygmy, or unusually short, people—a claim for which no evidence has yet been discovered. Trying to pry apart oral history from the many myths and legends of the Vazimba is close to impossible without corroborating evidence. Some traditions say the Vazimba died out at the hands of the more powerful and technologically advanced Merina culture; others suggest the first group simply became assimilated into the second group.

Antananarivo was originally a Vazimba town called Analamangao, but nothing much is known about the place or the vanished people who lived there. Today, small groups who are perhaps descended from the Vazimba do live in the rocky *tsingy*—an irregular limestone or dolomite landscape with sinkholes, underground streams, and caverns.

After the arrival of the original Vazimba, more settlers landed. In later years, those early inhabitants mixed with African slaves; Arab, Indian, and Portuguese traders; and also French colonials to form the ethnic groups of the island today.

ETHNIC GROUPS

The Malagasy are made up of about eighteen to twenty ethnic groups, all of whom speak the same language. These groups are largely people of mixed

descent whose members tend to marry among their own ethnicities. The rather vague boundaries of their homelands are based on the traditional boundaries of ancient kingdoms.

The largest such group is the Merina. They once ruled the island and even now represent about 24 percent of the population. Merina means "elevated people," and although most live on the high plateau around Antananarivo, they have also settled in other parts of the island. There used to be three social groups: nobles, freemen, and workers, but such categories are no longer used in democratic Madagascar, at least not officially. However, old designations of social status have survived over the years.

Another large group, making up approximately 13 percent of the population, is the Betsimisaraka, which literally means "inseparable multitude." The people were initially from several smaller indigenous groups that blended together. They settled along the east coast where they were subjected to the influence of Europeans, particularly eighteenth-century pirates who arrived by sailing ships. Highly superstitious, they believe in

Merina people carry provisions as they walk from one town to another in Fianarantsoa Province.

ghosts, mermaids, and little wild men from the forest that they refer to as *kalamoro* (KAR-la-MOOR).

The Betsileo, meaning "the invincibles," is the next largest group at about 11 percent, and they live on the central plateau south of Fianarantsoa and the region around Antananarivo. They are mainly rice growers and wood-carvers. Merina and Betsileo are mainly descendants of early Malayan and Indonesian immigrants.

Other important groups are the Tsimihety, meaning "those who do not cut their hair"; the Sakalava, "people of the long valley"; the Antandroy, "people of the thornbush"; the Tanala, "people of the forest"; the Antaimoro, "people of the banks"; and the Bara, whose name is of uncertain origin. Smaller groups include the Antanosy, the Antaifasy, the Sihanaka, the Antakarana, the Betanimena, the Bezanozano, and the Mahafaly.

GROWING POPULATION

Madagascar has an ethnically diverse population of about 24.4 million. There are four non-Malagasy minority groups: French, Chinese, Comorian, and an economically significant Indo-Pakistani community. The Comorian group is made up of primarily Muslim African-Arab people from the islands of Comoros, located some 544 miles (875 km) northwest of Madagascar. There used to be a larger community of Comorians on Madagascar, but after violent clashes and race riots, many retreated to the Comoro Islands in 1977.

Madagascar's population is predominantly young, rural, and poor. Some 60 percent of the people are under the age of twenty-five. Girls tend to marry and begin having children at a very young age—and despite widespread poverty, large families are common. The population, therefore, is growing rapidly, increasing at an average rate of 2.54 percent per year, one of the highest rates in the world. At this rate, the island's population is set to double every thirty years, which will increase pressure on the nation's available food, jobs, and other resources.

The Malagasy believe that children are gifts from God and must be welcomed. They believe that the more children one has, the greater is one blessed. It is quite normal for a family to have as many as eight or ten children, and fourteen is considered a lucky number.

A family with many children travel on an oxcart in Amnoromalandy.

DRESS

The all-purpose garment is the *lamba* (LAM-ba), a length of silk or cotton worn around the shoulders togalike and often draped over the head like a shawl. The way the *lamba* is draped around a woman indicates whether she

Antandroy men wear colorful lambas at the market in Itampolo in the south of Madagascar.

is single, married, or widowed. If one end hangs down the right side of the body, it indicates mourning. Along the west coast and in the far south women often also wear sarongs or loose skirts.

For the Merina people, the *lamba* is usually made of white cotton, and it is draped across the left shoulder like a Roman toga. Women of other groups, such as the Sakalava and Antakarana, wear colorful cotton *lambas* that they use for carrying babies while shopping or working in the fields.

Men also wear *lambas*, either around the waist or tied in a knot on the shoulder. On special occasions they may wear the long *lamba mena* (LAM-ba MAIN), meaning red cloth (although it is seldom red) indicating authority. *Lamba mena* also refers to the shroud used to wrap a dead body. Muslims wear the clothes indicated by Islamic tradition: men wear somber colors and usually a brimless cap, while married women are fully robed.

Often, another garment is worn under the *lamba*. Women may wear a long dress, and men may wear jeans or shorts that are nearly always paired with a hat, for hats are seen as a sign of respectability. Western-style clothes are common, too. Shorts, short-sleeved shirts, and dresses are typical everyday wear. The Betsileo wear four-cornered hats, the Merina favor rice-straw hats, and the Bara wear cone-shaped hats. Woven raffia hats are for sale in every market, and even the jaunty American baseball cap has made its way to Madagascar.

Although boys may wear nothing more than a pair of shorts, girls and women dress modestly, always covering their chests. Well-coifed hair is socially important. Some women grease their hair with animal fat to make it shine. Others tie their hair back with a colored ribbon. Well groomed hairstyles reflect happiness. When a person is in mourning, though, the hair is left to hang down uncombed and untidy.

INTERNET LINKS

https://www.britannica.com/place/Madagascar
Britannica's chapter on Madagascar includes information about ethnic groups and demographics.

https://www.cia.gov/library/publications/the-world-factbook/geos/ma.html
The *CIA World Factbook* provides up-to-date statistics about the Malagasy.

http://madagascar.opendataforafrica.org/gallery/Census-Data
The outdated but latest available census data from 1993 is available on this site.

https://phys.org/news/2016-07-island-history-human-genetic-ancestry.html
This and other related short articles on this science site explore the origins of the Malagasy people.

LIFESTYLE

A little girl carries her younger brother in Antananarivo.

7

MADAGASCAR IS A POOR COUNTRY, and its people's lifestyle reflects this fact. There is a vast difference between the lifestyles of those few with money and those many without. The rich live in the same way the French did when the island was still a French colony; others eat only what they can grow or obtain by barter. An estimated 65 percent of Malagasy live in the countryside growing rice, tending cattle, or doing other farming-related activities. Urban residents make up slightly more than a third of the population.

TOWN LIFE

The hilltops around Antananarivo are ringed by huge circles. These are the deep defensive ditches that once guarded fortified villages, some of which had gates made of solid wheels of stone. Present-day villagers do not need to defend themselves, and many have moved down the hillsides to be nearer to potable water. But some inhabitants are still wary of the outside world.

Madagascar scored 158 out of 188 countries on the Human Development Index (HDI) for 2016, which places it in the lowest category. (For comparison, Norway ranked first and Central African Republic, last.) This annual assessment by the United Nations Development Programme determines a country's average achievement in three categories of human experience— having a long and healthy life, being knowledgeable, and having a decent standard of living.

At the Analakely Market in the capital city, taxis wait for customers at a taxi stand in October 2016.

The biggest city in Madagascar is the nation's capital, Antananarivo. Not only is it the center of government, education, and the economy, it is also the capital of the region of Analamanga. The city fans outward; houses are built on hills and ridges, and fields cover the floor of every valley. The inhabitants consider themselves city dwellers, even though some may plant rice and make sun-dried mud bricks. Taxis and telephones, newspapers and schools, freshly baked bread (long, thin baguettes in the French style), and machinery are all easily accessible and available. Shops offer art, jewelry, cameras, and computers as in any other city in the world.

Richer families live in the Upper Town where the more expensive stores are located. Narrow streets alive with traffic twist their way between blocks of shops and houses two or three stories high. On the lower slopes is a sea of red walls, terra-cotta roof tiles, and rusty iron rooftops. An occasional white minaret and several church spires spring up in between.

Near the bright flowers and green lawns of the Place de l'Indépendence ("Independence Place") stand most of the governmental buildings, including the impressive President's Palace. The military guards, wearing scarlet berets, have sentry boxes painted with stripes of white, green, and red. ShopRite, the best supermarket in town, with a wide array of food, clothing, and imported goods, is also there.

The highest hill is crowned with the old Queen's Palace, called the Rova, which was gutted by a fire in 1995. There is also a miniature Greek temple that seems curiously out of place. The twisting road that plunges down the hillside passes tiny shops.

Brightly colored plastic, which does not rot, is replacing the soft, natural colors of wood in the towns. The capital city may be crowded, dusty, shabby, and busy, yet those who live in it are the lucky ones. They have easier access to health resources—although those are limited—and most of their children attend school.

COUNTRY LIVING

Much of Madagascar's countryside may seem remote and isolated. Whether people live beside lagoons, in the mountains, forests, or fields, the lack of roads and telephones make communication very difficult. But underneath the simplicity of living in the rural regions is the resilient drive of their inhabitants. The Malagasy are committed to earning enough to survive. They may lead cattle to nearly dried-up water holes, pick and sort vanilla

A fishing village hugs the banks of the Pangalenes Canal.

pods, paddle dugout canoes in search of fish, or offer handfuls of nuts to potential buyers. Farmers, involved with the yearlong cycle of rice growing, guide cattle around the fields to plow the mud. They then plant the rice seedlings, bending over flooded fields, tend to and weed the crop, and scythe the harvest. After that comes the work of pounding the rice in a wooden mortar. Most families grow only enough for their own needs but often have to sell part of that to obtain cash.

At the southern tip of the island, village people typically live in huts made of wood and leaves. The men work on a nearby sisal plantation or fish the lake in pirogues made of baobab wood. Their nets, which are hung out on trees to dry, use stones for weights and carved baobab wood, which is very light, for floats.

While the women sift through the tangled, spiny scrub for edible roots, the children play on the water's edge, careful not to touch the poisonous pink jellyfish. Older youngsters keep an eye on their family's few chickens, goats, and pigs.

What good timber remains in Madagascar is under constant attack. In the absence of mechanized tools, woodcutters often use old methods. A two-man team will cut a trunk into planks, one man guiding the long saw from a high platform, the other below, pulling—and finding himself covered in sawdust. It is a hard way to earn a living.

Charcoal-burners use eucalyptus wood (the eucalyptus tree was introduced to replace the fast-disappearing forests), piling logs into stacks and leaving them to smoulder under a cover of turf sods for a week. The resulting sacks of charcoal may be the only source of income for a whole village.

In some communities the village is the woman's place and the forest is the man's; so it is a man's job to collect wood and a woman's task to use it for cooking.

A Malagasy boy carries branches on his head.

FAMILY LIFE

The extended family has traditionally been the strength of Malagasy society. A family council that included the grandparents used to make decisions pertaining to children's upbringing, basing decisions on ideals such as family solidarity, respect for elders, and mutual help. Much of this has changed, however, and many Malagasy say that family life in the past was better than what it is now, the young were more respectful, and there was greater harmony. Today, the generational differences are being felt, and traditional family structure may not be able to withstand a more modern lifestyle.

As divorce is now fairly common, Madagascar has an increasing number of single-parent families. The old ideal of having "seven boys and seven girls" is proving difficult to accomplish. With a growing number of broken homes, children are sometimes sent out to work, and some become unfortunate victims of abuse.

Madagascar is also not spared the prevalent and worrying trend of modernized living as evident in many other parts of the world. Even when the family is intact, parents have to work and are often not around to impart social values to their children. This increasing lack of communication is a prime cause of delinquency. Children left to their own devices may soon discover the world of drugs and petty crime. Many parents try to cope with this situation by adopting highly repressive and punitive attitudes, leading to conflict within the home.

CATTLE

Several hundred years ago, African humpback zebu cattle were introduced to Madagascar. Today, a herd of these cattle represents a walking bank account advertising the owner's wealth and respectability. A person's importance in the local society is measured in cattle.

When a man manages to earn more money, he buys more cattle. Putting money in a bank is not a popular idea. Yet the cattle's significance extends beyond wealth. The well-being of the herds of a village stands for the continuing health and prosperity of the whole group of people who own them. Fat humps show that the cattle are in peak condition—but quantity is still considered

more important than quality! Since cattle are such an established sign of wealth, it is not surprising that cattle rustlers (people who steal cattle) are afoot, especially in the savannah plains of the west and the dry south.

More than eighty words in the Malagasy language describe the people's beloved cattle and every part of their horns, hump, and hide. Cows come in various colors, and each color means something different. White muzzles, for example, look like restricting nosebags, so the owner of cows with such muzzles is said to be unlikely to find prosperity. A dappled hide denotes uncertainty, whereas a hide all of one color—except black, as pure black means ruin, like black fields devastated by locusts—indicates solidarity. Black-and-white cattle seem safer.

Cattle are occasionally sacrificed to please the ancestors and are sold or sacrificed if someone is very ill, as an offering to make that person well again. After a funeral, horns will be put on the grave to show how many zebus were slaughtered for the feast and thereby how rich and important the deceased had been.

DAILY SURVIVAL

Poverty is rife in the country and much remains to be done to address still persistent unemployment, housing scarcity, homelessness, rural education, and health-care problems. Governmental reforms have not yet relieved these conditions.

In parts of the parched countryside that receive no rain for seven or eight months in a row, survival is a life skill for both people and plants. Spiky plants and succulents have found a way to live, and as well, humans have learned to survive. There seems hardly anywhere to live or anything to live on, and for many months of the year, it may be too hot to work. Still, people carry firewood, water, vegetables, logs, and bulging sacks of rice in the hope of making a sale whenever they can. However, when drought aggravates this already dry situation, as it did in 2016—2017, it can easily push the fragile population over the line into famine.

TRANSPORTATION PROBLEMS

"Madagascar is not an island but an archipelago." This local saying emphasizes the diversity of the people and the poor means of communication, as if groups were isolated little islands in a chain. As part of their defense strategy, several pre-colonial kingdoms refused to build roads. Even today it seems as if the Malagasy do not want better roads because that might invite an invasion of people. Most trails are made of dirt or mud and are almost unusable after a rain. One favored Malagasy word is *mandrevou* (MAND-dr-FOH), which means "bottomless mud." The few paved roads that exist are pocked with potholes, and road signs are unknown. This condition is improving, though, as many important roads are now in the process of being paved. Most travelers travel by air or "port hop" around the coast by boat.

Much of the street traffic consists of carts pulled by two zebu oxen roped to a wooden yoke, ramshackle bicycles, or sometimes a car or van. But there are two vehicles that are special to Madagascar. The first is the *pousse-pousse* (POOSS-POOSS) meaning "push-push," a cart for passengers or goods, pulled

Frontières (Doctors without Borders) have made free medical care and follow-up available to thousands of street children. The organization has been working in Madagascar since 1987 and is currently engaged in projects to improve sanitary conditions.

In the countryside, Western medicine remains expensive and difficult to obtain. Many people still trust in traditional medicine that has been handed down through the generations. The rain forests are full of medicinal plants used in herbal treatments. The *raraha* (RA-rah) plant, for example, has anesthetic qualities and is used to ease sore gums and toothache. People in the countryside believe that illness may have more than a physical cause and that a healer does not cure the illness alone, but the whole person. The traditional healer is called the *ombiasy* (om-bi-ASH) and ministers by means of invocations or magic chanting, with perhaps an animal sacrifice and a pinch of herbs.

INTERNET LINKS

https://www.csmonitor.com/World/Africa/2017/0725/Madagascar-skirted-famine-barely.-Now-it-s-boosting-resilience-before-drought-returns
This in-depth article examines drought and famine in Madagascar and the efforts being made to help the people survive.

http://hdr.undp.org/en
The UNDP Human Development Reports are found on this site.

http://www.unfpa.org/sites/default/files/jahia-publications/documents/publications/2012/ChildMarriage_2_chapter1.pdf
This UN report explains and documents child marriage around the world.

http://www.who.int/gho/countries/mdg/country_profiles/en
The World Health Organization country profile on Madagascar covers a range of health topics.

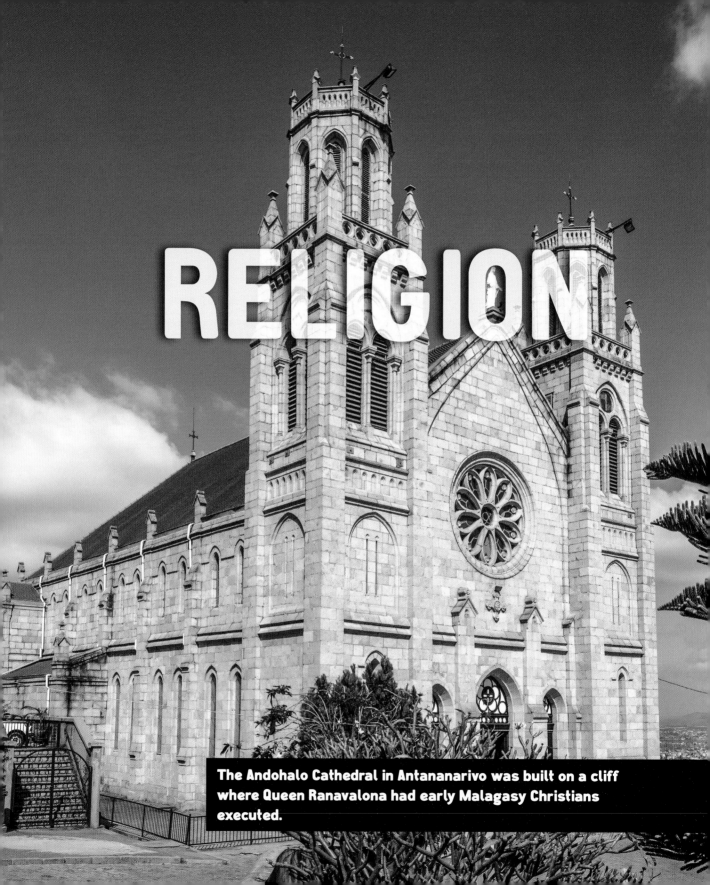

RELIGION

The Andohalo Cathedral in Antananarivo was built on a cliff where Queen Ranavalona had early Malagasy Christians executed.

THE MALAGASY REGARD THEIR country as the sacred land of their ancestors, who perpetually remain its rightful owners. Many people go to church, but that does not stop them from making sacrifices to their ancestors. Christianity is practiced hand in hand with traditional beliefs; it has not taken their place.

ORGANIZED RELIGION

The Christian faith has existed in Madagascar ever since King Radama I encouraged British missionaries to come in the early nineteenth century. They opened schools and chapels, produced the first dictionary of the Malagasy language, translated the Bible into Malagasy, and converted many to Christianity. The London Missionary Society introduced Protestant Christianity, but as French influence increased, so too did Roman Catholicism. The Protestant churches are found mainly in the highlands today, largely supported by the Merina people, while the more numerous Catholics are located mostly near the coast, where they enjoy support from the Betsileo people. Protestant and Catholic churches often compete for new adherents, and it is not unusual to find at least two churches in the central highland communities, one Protestant and one Roman Catholic, facing each other at opposite ends of the village.

8

A large number of Western Christian ministries operate in Madagascar. Although they represent various denominations, their goal is the same—to convert the Malagasy to Christianity and to dissuade them from following their indigenous beliefs. The missionaries consider non-Christian Malagasy to be "unreached." Many of these missionary groups also provide significant aid, education, and other services to the very poor people of the island.

This 1865 illustration pictures the massacre of Christians on Madagascar in 1849.

Radama's widow was called the Wicked Queen and the Mad Queen of Madagascar. During her thirty-three-year reign (1828—1861), Queen Ranavallona prohibited Christian practices, killed those who disobeyed, and forced missionaries to leave. Churches built of stone in Antananarivo stand in remembrance of Madagascar's first Christian martyrs. One inscription reads, "Erected by the London Missionary Society in memory of twelve individuals who died in or near Madagascar in endeavoring to introduce on the island the blessings of civilization and the knowledge of the glorious gospel of the Blessed God."

About 45 percent of the population is Christian (about 25 percent Protestant and 20 percent Roman Catholic) and 7 percent are Muslim. The majority of Muslims are found in Mahajanga, a breezy town on the northwest coast of Madagascar. Most are Comorian or Indo-Pakistani, while a small number are converted Malagasy. The rest of the population practice traditional beliefs.

TRADITIONAL WORSHIP AND DESTINY

The earliest Malagasy believed in a supreme being as well as secondary deities or spirits that inhabited waters, trees, and stones. They also respected creatures such as snakes, crocodiles, and lemurs, and held that humans have spirits that do not die after bodily death.

Even today, the people believe strongly in their ancestors' power to influence disasters (such as famine, drought, and cyclones), as well as happiness, prosperity, and luck. The dead are not regarded as having departed for good but are believed to remain with the family and play as important a role as they did when they were alive. Therefore they must be honored, consulted, pleased, and asked to bestow good fortune on the family. A family may throw a party in honor of an ancestor. Each clan has its own beliefs, and practices different ways of burying their dead. An ancestor's soul can die if it is left out of the thoughts of its relatives. At village gatherings people ask for their ancestors' permission to hold the meeting. Nobody is thought to be "dead and gone."

From such customs arise the idea of personal fate or destiny, called *vintana*, and the conviction that certain actions are *fady* (FAH-di), forbidden or taboo, because they bring bad luck. Belief in *vintana* is particularly strong in the coastal areas exposed to Islamic influence. Those people believe that there are certain times of high and low fortune, which are foretold in the stars according to the moment of one's birth. So there are good or bad *vintana* periods. By choosing the "best times" for birth, marriage, or burial, people can prevent accidents, illnesses, and trouble. The choice of a marriage partner is complicated by *vintana*. Every person is said to represent one of the basic elements of water, fire, wind, or hill. Wind cannot marry hill; fire can marry wind, but if fire marries water the fire will be put out.

Days of the week carry their own vintana. Monday is not a good day for work and can bring sorrow, but it is a good day for undertaking projects as they will last (such as building a house). Tuesday is an easy day, bad for important agreements but good for light work, travel, and having fun. Wednesday is "the day of poor return," so if one plants on that day, there will be a poor harvest and, even more alarming, if one goes traveling, one

A crowd of mourners follows a traditional funeral procession in Isalo.

is wrapped in an expensive shroud and buried, with the head facing east and the feet facing west, in whatever style is used in that region. In the west and on the plateau, children do not inherit their father's cattle. When he dies, his herd of cattle is slaughtered and their horns displayed on the tomb to show his importance.

Not everyone is entitled to a burial. Among the Antaisaka people of Mananjary, twins were historically killed or abandoned in the forest after birth. Such an act is now against the law, but the superstition against twins still persists, and they may not be buried in a tomb. Suspected sorcerers are dumped to the west of their village, their necks twisted so that they face south, and their bodies left in the open for wild animals to feed on.

All Malagasy names have meanings. When a person dies, relatives choose a new name for the deceased that highlights his or her good qualities—for

FADY

Whether it is based on hope or fear, religion or superstition, the belief in fady *rules most aspects of daily living. Such beliefs have endless variations. Customs or behavior forbidden in one place may be allowed in another only a few miles away. In one village, for example, it may be fady to eat pork, while a neighboring village is filled with squealing pigs.*

Fady greatly affects the vital rice crop. Rice represents the toil of countless ancestors, and so it is holy. It may be fady, therefore, to move stones or building materials near the field because the noise might disturb the rice. It is also fady to sit in the doorway of a house while the rice is beginning to sprout, as it will impede the growth of the rice. Bad weather may also destroy the crop if anyone dares to gather marsh grass for matting at the time of planting.

It may be fady to sing while eating, or to whistle on a certain stretch of beach, or to walk past a sacred tree. Feathers are fady for bedding or pillows because they symbolize flight, and thus might impede a stable and grounded home life. Instead, mattresses are stuffed with chopped straw. Fady also determines the direction in which one lies down to sleep. Men usually sleep with their heads to the north, which represents power, and their wives and children with their heads to the east, regarded as sacred. No one sleeps with feet to the east in case the person kicks the sunrise. In all things, ancestors must be respected. The prohibitions of fady are obeyed by tradition to prevent causing offense to anyone or anything and suffering bad luck and misfortune as a result. As fady differs from place to place, foreigners are generally exempted from observing these taboos. Nevertheless, it's considerate to be mindful to avoid offending the local people.

example, "He who made work look easy" or "The woman who did her duty." Any living relative who has the same name as the deceased's newly acquired one must change his or her name, as it is *fady* to use the same name. The widow in mourning, according to Sakavala custom, dresses in old clothes and remains in the house. She does not speak to anyone except close relatives. When the period of mourning (which can be several weeks) is over, she will dress in clean clothes, come out of the house, and speak to people to signify her return to the normal world.

The Malagasy esteem for ancestors is expressed in the extraordinary ritual of famadihana (fa-ma-dee-an). It is practiced mainly by the Merina and Betsileo people on the high plateau and is regarded as a duty that the living owe to the deceased. This involves opening the tomb, removing the old lamba that acted as a shroud, washing and rewrapping the body in a fine new silk shroud, and then replacing it reverently back in the tomb. Since the ancestors are not thought to have departed and their spirits are very much alive, they must be welcomed, talked to, and entertained. What is important is to show that they have not been forgotten, and family members may even hug them or dance with them. Tears and lamentation will not please the deceased.

The famadihana can last for up to a week, which means that the family will have to hire a band, employ an officiating ombiasy, sacrifice cattle, and pay for food and refreshments. Women who are trying to conceive may take small pieces of the old burial shroud. When put under their mattresses, these pieces of cloth are said to induce fertility. Even devout Christians may take part in the whole ritual. Depending on the family's wealth, the ceremony is held every third, fifth, or seventh year, but only during the dry season, between June and September.

Churches may frown on famadihana but have not attempted to forbid it because the custom is so deeply rooted in the lifestyle of the people. It is a principal source of their loyalty to their hometown or village, signifies their attachment to their tribal group, and demonstrates their respect for older people and the deceased. There are signs, however, that the practice is waning, partly because it is not in keeping with church custom, but mainly because of its cost.

Throughout the island, each tribe handles funerals and burial rites in its own way. The common factor is that all want their tombs to be more permanent than their houses. Those tombs might be in the shape of stone mausoleums, cave tombs, underground chambers with stone shelves, or walled enclosures that are painted. Other structures are sometimes used in place of tombs: long rows of stones with crosses mounted on them, carved wooden totem poles in the shape of people and animals, or obelisks marked only with a name (in which case the burial place is elsewhere, its location kept secret). The most elaborate tombs are those constructed by the Mahafaly people in the south, using intricately carved upright pillars that depict scenes from the person's life with sculptures and inscriptions. Sorrow belongs on the "cold" south side of a village, so tombs are usually sited there and built only at night. The shadow of a tomb must not touch the homes of the living.

INTERNET LINKS

http://www.cnn.com/2016/10/18/travel/madagascar-turning-bones/index.html
This CNN travel article about famadihana includes videos.

http://www.madamagazine.com/en/fady
This article explains fady, and provides links to related topics about Madagascar.

http://www.nytimes.com/2010/09/06/world/africa/06madagascar.html?pagewanted=all&mcubz=0
This *New York Times* article provides a first-person account of a famadihana ritual.

LANGUAGE

A street sign on a rural road in Sandrandahy is written in French.

9

LIKE THE PEOPLE THEMSELVES, THE language of Madagascar is called Malagasy. And like the people's DNA—their distinctive genetic code—this language is like an old treasure map that pinpoints their historic origins. Malagasy is almost as unique as its rare lemurs, chameleons, and orchids. Related to the Malayo-Polynesian family of languages spoken in the Malay Peninsula, with the addition of some words from Africa (Bantu languages and Kiswahili) and Arabia, Malagasy is a blend of Asia and Africa, with features not found anywhere else in the world.

GROWTH OF A LANGUAGE

In a country where the skills of reading and writing are still not universal, the spoken word remains highly important. The Malagasy language derived from Indonesia is remarkably uniform throughout the island. Although there are numerous regional variations, they are all linguistically related to the same Malagasy language.

Kabary ("public discourse") is a style of eloquent ceremonial speaking through indirect speech that uses proverbs and metpahors. One who is skilled in kabary is a *mpikabary*. This style of discourse can be performed as a competition, where two speakers debate with each other but can never directly counter one another. Men are usually the masters of kabary while women are expected to speak more literally.

The Antaimoro were the first people in Madagascar to adopt writing. Their holy men traveled widely throughout the country, adding an Islamic influence to the local language. Malagasy still uses Arabic-derived names for days of the week and months of the year. It also contains adopted words from English, French, and other tongues. As the first missionaries were British, Malagasy words relating to religion, education, or anything literary often have an English base, whereas anything to do with food or drink tends to be French-related, and words dealing with cattle and domestic animals come from the Kiswahili spoken in Africa.

ORAL TRADITIONS

Hainteny ("knowledge of words") is a traditional form of Malagasy oral literature and poetry involving heavy use of metaphor. The use of playful language is introduced in the early years, as children learn the symbolic importance of question-and-answer through the basic word game of riddling. Through learning to appreciate metaphor, they find that language is ambiguous. Here are some of their riddles:

"God's stick has water in its stomach." (sugarcane)

"Five men with round hats." (fingers)

"White chicks filling a hole." (teeth in mouth)

Wordplay is thus common in everyday talk and in Malagasy proverbs. For instance, "Darken the mouth of the cooking pot" is frequently used to describe dusk.

The mastery of unhurried speaking in public, called *kabary* (ka-BAHR), is still very much a part of Malagasy culture. Village elders can speak for hours, using witty double meanings, riddles, and complicated proverbs. It is a traditional skill, used especially at weddings and funerals. It is also widely used in daily talk, even if the younger folk do not have much time for it nowadays. The speakers delight in using more words than may be necessary. When asked how far away a particular place is, a Malagasy might answer, "A person walking fairly fast will probably reach there in the time it takes to cook a pot of rice."

WRITTEN RECORDS

In European literature, the earliest mention of Madagascar appears to have been made by Marco Polo in the thirteenth century. He wrote, "You must know that this island is one of the biggest and best in the whole world." He may have confused the island with Mogadishu in Somalia, however, because one of the spelling forms he used was Mogdaxo.

Other theories on the meaning of Madagascar are "Island of Ghosts" and "Island of Ancestors." Visiting Arabs called Madagascar "The Island of the Moon." The Malagasy themselves use terms such as "The Great Island," "The Red Island," or "The Happy Island."

Among Marco Polo's mixture of reported truths and fictions was the mention of a giant bird that he called a gryphon and that the islanders called a *rukh* (ROOK), or "roc" in English. A giant bird also appears one of the tales of the *Arabian Nights*, in which Sinbad the Sailor refers to a huge roc that can "truss elephants in its talons." Could this have been Madagascar's now-extinct elephant bird?

Radama I, who was given the title of "king" by Sir Robert Farquhar, British governor of Mauritius, sent out a request for missionaries to help with Madagascar's education and development. In 1817, two of those sent by the London Missionary Society were Welshmen David Jones and David Griffiths. With help from the king, they set about recording the Malagasy language in the European (Latin) alphabet. Phonetically, the language was almost perfectly consistent, with the consonants pronounced as in English and the vowels as in French. The first school was set up, and by 1835 the Bible was printed in Malagasy. Today it remains a language that is more spoken than written, very much a living language.

Did the Venetian traveler Marco Polo (1254-1324) visit Madagascar? Historians aren't certain. Here, he is pictured circa 1300.

A little boy practices his handwriting.

LANGUAGE DILEMMA

One problem often encountered in developing countries is whether to teach children in their mother tongue or a First World language. In 1972 Malagasy replaced French as the medium of instruction in schools in the hope of making education more accessible to all. But to be literate in a language used only on one island in the world does not help international communications. So in 1986, French was reintroduced in secondary schools. It is now the language of instruction in all schools and is used for literary, business, and administrative purposes. It is functional but not very popular with the people; a qualified schoolteacher may teach in French and English, yet think in Malagasy.

Malagasy remains the spoken language throughout the island. English, which used to be spoken only to tourists, is now regarded as desirable for business transactions. To further cement the growing importance of the language, Madagascar has adopted English as an unofficial third language. Among the many notices posted in Malagasy outside a church, which acts as a village's social center, there may be a flyer in French announcing the activities of the local "English Club," offering villagers the opportunity to learn to speak English "without hesitation" and to become a "man of affairs or tourist guide." Madagascar also has one English-language newspaper, published by the English Speaking Union, called the *Madagascar News*. Newspapers like *L'Express*, *Les Nouvelles*, *Madagascar Tribune*, *Gazette de la Grande Ile,* and *Midi Madagasikara* are mainly in French, as indicated by their names, but have columns in Malagasy.

People view a wide array of newspapers for sale in the city.

In Antananarivo, French is spoken as often as Malagasy. In rural areas, however, it may be resented as a colonial language, so people use Malagasy at home, French in school, and English on the beer bottles—labeled Three Horses Beer, even though there are very few horses in Madagascar.

Since Madagascar gained its independence from France in 1960, many towns have reverted to their original names. Here are some of the old Malagasy and colonial French names:

Malagasy	French
Mahajanga	Majunga
Antsiranana	Diégo-Suarez
Nosy Boraha	Sainte Marie
Toamasina	Tamatave
Toliara	Tuléar
Tôla¨naro	Fort Dauphin

Most people seem happy enough that the island itself is still called Madagascar, although in the Malagasy language it is Madagasikara.

Hello . . . . *Manao ahoana* (mano OHN)

What's new? . . . . *Inona no vaovao?* (EE-nan vow-vow)

No news . . . . *Tsy misy* (tsee MEESS)

Please/Excuse me . . . . . *Aza fady* (a-za FAAD)

Thank you . . . . *Misaotra* (mis-OW-tr)

Good-bye . . . . *Veloma* (ve-LOOM)

HOW TO SAY THE WORDS

The Malagasy alphabet has twenty-one letters. The following letters are not used: *c*, *q*, *u*, *w*, and *x*; *c* is replaced by *s* or *k*, and *x* with *ks*. The letter *o* is usually pronounced like *oo*, so *veloma*, meaning good-bye, is pronounced "ve-LOOM." The stress is usually on the penultimate syllable, although vowels that come at the end of a word are sometimes not pronounced at all. For example, *sifaka* is pronounced "SHE-fak." A general rule seems to be, "swallow as many syllables as you can and drop the last one." Sometimes the way one says a word changes its meaning—*tanana* (TAN-an-a) means "hand," but *tanána* (written with an accent and pronounced ta-NA-na) means "town." In general, though, the Malagasy language has no accents. Words with diacritics, or accent marks, are of French origin.

Malagasy is a poetic language. For example, the term for the early hours of the morning is translated "when the wild cat washes itself." Names of people and places also have meanings. Antananarivo, the capital, means "city of the thousand" because it is said that a thousand warriors originally guarded it. Words are often joined together (as in Welsh or German) to create long personal and place names. For example, people think nothing of pronouncing the name of the island's most famous king, Andrianampoinimerinandriantsimitoviaminandriampanjaka, without drawing a breath.

GREETINGS

Greeting a friend is a serious affair and must not be hurried. The traditional Malagasy greeting is to take an offered hand between one's own hands. Those who are more modern copy the French fashion, kissing three times on alternate cheeks, but they like to shake hands, too.

Salama (sal-AHM), a greeting in some coastal regions, is a variation of the Arabic *salaam*. The more common greeting is *manao ahoana* (mano OHN). Europeans are not called "white" because the color white is considered offensive; "white" refers to all that is ugly and of low quality, and an unreliable person is one who speaks "white words." So visitors are called *vazaha* (va-ZAH), or foreigner. The Malagasy are extremely courteous and do not speak loudly or shout. They do not speak lightly of old people or death.

INTERNET LINKS

http://www.omniglot.com/writing/malagasy.htm
Omniglot gives a good introduction to Malagasy with videos and links.

http://www.wildmadagascar.org/people/malagasy-english.html
A Malagasy-English phrasebook is provided here, but no pronunciation guides.

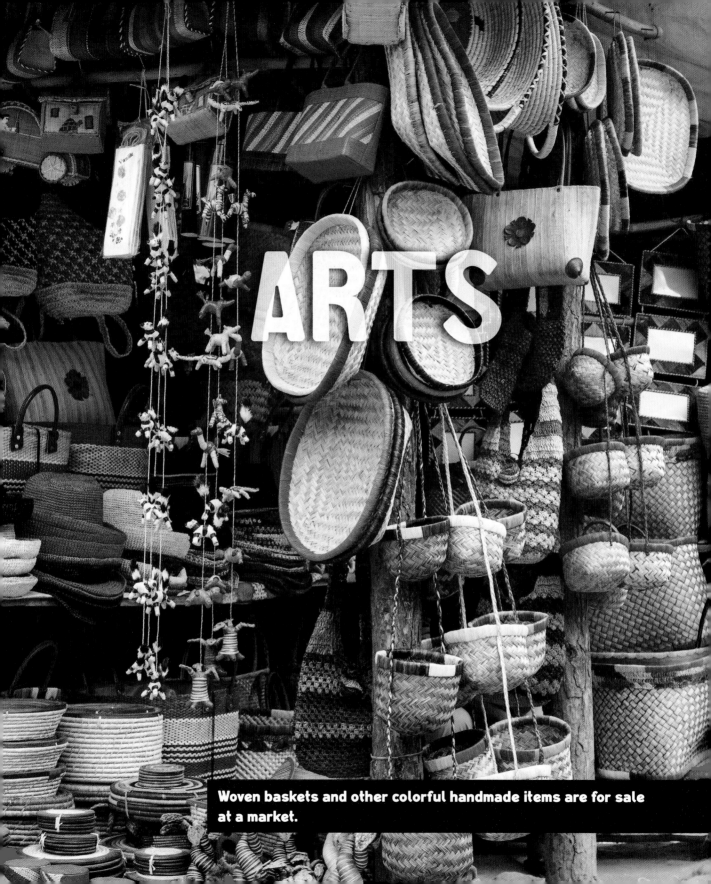

ARTS

Woven baskets and other colorful handmade items are for sale at a market.

10

THE MALAGASY ARE CLOSE TO nature. The artist, sculptor, wood-carver, or painter does not try to create an imitation of the world around him. His world is one in which a creator God has given the spirit of life to everything—humans, animals, plants, and stones alike. Even the deceased retain their spirit. So any work of art must be so beautiful that it pleases the spirit for whom it is intended and perhaps attracts the spirit to live in or feel associated with it. Even music is often something created out of emotion generated by a special moment.

For most poor people, an object's worth or beauty is judged by its usefulness. So weavers make cloth to wear or hats for shade; embroiderers make tablecloths or collars; and wood-carvers make tomb adornments in wood. Such tomb decorations acquire a sacred quality as well.

In the capital city of Antananarivo, there are museums of history, art, and archaeology, as well as the National Library. The Albert Camus Cultural Center is used for many concerts and film showings, while branches of the Alliance Française in Antananarivo and around the

Music is a sacred part of the Malagasy daily life. Music is believed to be the connection to an ancestor's soul, and sometimes at parties and celebrations, rum is poured into the instruments as a show of respect for the dead.

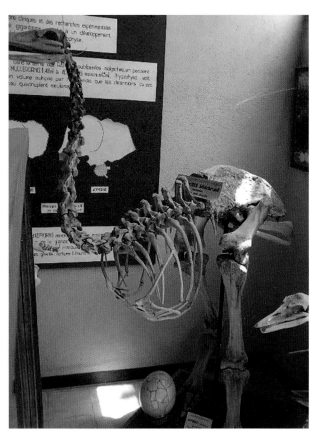

The skeleton of an extinct elephant bird is on display at the Tsimbazaza Zoo.

country stage cultural events. There is national pride in the country's cultural history. The restoration of the burned-down Queen's Palace in Antananarivo, for example, has drawn support from several provincial councils, notably those of Toliara and Toamasina, as well as that of the capital itself. There is also generous support from the German government.

Tsimbazaza Zoo includes displays of dinosaur bones and elephant bird eggs, and a terrarium of indigenous reptiles. The zoo also houses an ethnographic museum that showcases the cultures and peoples of the island.

LITERATURE

The most popular use of language in Madagascar is oral; there is a long tradition of oratory, known as *kabary* (ka-BAHR), which includes speech making and storytelling. Originating with the tribal councils of elders, this linguistic skill has been extended from political polemic to sheer entertainment. A masterful speaker spins a web around his subject, referring to it in clever metaphors and intricate proverbs and references, never coming directly to the point, to the delight of his audience. Such linguistic prowess is greatly admired.

Proverbs are rich and popular, combining wisdom and wit, as in the following examples.

> "You can trap an ox by its horns and a man by his words."
> "The man who refuses to buy a lid for the pot will eat badly cooked rice."
> "If you are only a dung beetle, don't try to move mountains."
> "Invite a big eater and he will finish the meal; advise a fool and he will waste your time."

Writing was first introduced to Madagascar by the Antaimoro people during the reign of King Andrianampoinimerina at the end of the eighteenth century. The Antaimoro people, who possibly came from the Arabian Peninsula, settled near the Matitane River in the southeast around the end of the fifteenth century. They were the only keepers of religious texts that contained writings known as Sorabé. Based on an Arabic script, they are filled with prayers, magic formulas, genealogies, memorable events, and legends. These texts were held in great awe, and the Antaimoro's ability to write also gave them power and prestige throughout the land.

The Malagasy words were written on paper embedded with pressed dried flowers. The paper was made by using pulp from the *avoha* tree, and ink was extracted from the gum tree. The words were in an Arabic script so ancient that no one can decipher them today. This was the only form of writing in Madagascar until the first missionaries arrived. Unfortunately, the zealous considered the Sorabé books to be products of witchcraft and burned all that they could find.

There is scant famous Malagasy writing, perhaps due to the lack of diffusion, apart from the patriotic poetry of Jean-Joseph Rabearivelo, Jacques Rabemananjara, and Flavien Raniavo. Other poets known in Madagascar are Justin Rainizababololona, one of the first published Malagasy; Bruno Rahaingo, whose poems are politically engaged; and Ny Malodohasaha, whose writings coincided with the fall of the First Republic. The town of Fianarantsoa, an early center of learning, has gained a name as the island's contemporary literary capital. A number of writers have published their works there, among whom Emilson D. Andriamalala is probably the best known.

Moreover, there is a traditional style of love poetry perfected by the Merina called *hainteny* (HAY-ten-i). This can be soulful and profound, or somewhat more playful, as shown in this translation that is part of a series of questions with answers that have to be read between the lines.

> "What will you say you love me like?"
> "I love you like rice."
> "Then you love me not, for you only keep it stored up for
> when you are hungry."

Legends are featured prominently in Madagascar's oral tradition. One of the many favorite tales is that of the voronjaza *(voo-ROON-jahz) bird, or sickle-billed vanga.*

The story is set in a time of raiding pirates and slave traders. A mother and her child took refuge in the thick forest. Raiders who were close by heard a baby crying and headed toward the sound, laughing cruelly and anticipating with delight what they would find. Then they heard the sound again, but at that moment the voronjaza *hopped onto the branch of a tree and gave its call, which sounded just like the cry of a newborn baby. The pirates cursed the fact that they had been fooled by a bird and sailed away.*

The mother, however, knew that the bird had saved her child's life, for the first wail from her baby had been real enough. So the voronjaza *remains honored, and to this day it is* fady, *forbidden, to kill a* voronjaza.

Books are extremely expensive in Madagascar. The country has few libraries and even fewer bookshops. The selection of English-language books outside of the capital is limited, as most books come from France. The French comic book stories of Asterix are available, alongside French novels and magazines. A few Christian books in Malagasy are printed on cheap paper by missionary societies.

Newspapers are a different matter. In Antananarivo alone, there are three daily newspapers all printed in red and black and sold by newsboys on the street to people on their way to work or at popular vendor stands.

MUSIC

Music is a part of most people's lives, although traditional styles and rhythms have often been invaded by Western pop music. The Malagasy, especially the men, like singing in harmony. Many of the songs are church hymns because Malagasy social life often revolves around a church, but the singers love folk songs, too, sung in styles influenced by music from Polynesia to East Africa.

Local instruments include a cone-shaped drum of Indonesian origin and the *valiha* (va-LEE-a). This is similar to a zither, with twenty-one or more strings attached lengthways around a hollow bamboo tube. If the strings are attached to a rectangular sound box, it is called a *marovany* (MAH-ro-VAN). The instrument looks like a bassoon but is played like a harp to produce rippling chords. Expert players of the valiha include Tombo Daniel from Toamasina and Rakotozafy, who has recorded valiha music.

Many traditional instruments, made of bamboo or a gourd, produce only one note, such as the *kiloloka* (KEE-lo-LOOK) that whistles shrilly or the traditional Malagasy flute, the *sodina* (so-DEEN). Music is often made by a group of players producing harmonies and rhythmic variations as each

Musicians play on a sunny day in Antananarivo.

HIRA GASY

This traditional performance entertainment (pronounced HEE-ra GASH) is the Sunday showpiece of Antananarivo, and is seen only in the highlands. The actors usually perform at funerals and family celebrations, although traveling groups also tour villages and perform in community centers. Usually held in an open-air arena, it combines oratory, group opera, and dance.

A performance, which occupies most of the day, is a competition between two well-rehearsed groups of men and women on a central stage who take turns. They wear nineteenth-century French court dress—the men in military coats and the women in evening dress with silk lambas *around their shoulders.*

First comes the kabary, *which is a plea made by a skilled speaker to excuse his inadequacy, to praise God, and to welcome the rowdy audience. Then the* hira gasy *troupe performs a morality play that is sung and gestured, advising people to behave well in life so that they might go on to become good ancestors. Finally, synchronized dancers perform to the music of trumpets, drums, and violins. The teams alternate their performances, appealing to the crowd for their favor. Winners are judged by audience response and the applause generated.*

musician contributes his single note. The most famous player of the sodina is Rakotofra.

The African cultural influence is evident in the many drums, rattles, and sounding animal horns commonly played. There are guitars and fiddles, too. The more contemporary popularity of the accordion reflects the recent French colonial era.

The best-known Malagasy musician is probably Paul Rahasimanana, called Rossy, who earned his fame by performing *vaky soava* (vahk SOOV), choral music with a strong beat accompanied by hand clapping. He added instrumental accompaniment—his favorite insturment is the accordion—and soon became popular, playing in concerts and on the radio. In the 1980s his band toured Europe and the United States. His most famous recording was *Island of Ghosts* (1991), which seems a fitting theme for a place so bound up in its respect for the dead. In this piece of music, Rossy combines traditional styles with modern lyrics on the enduring themes of poverty, hope, and love. Rossy, together with other Malagasy artists, including D'Gary and Tovo, is also featured in the highly acclaimed music album *A World Out of Time*. The album was a result of their 1991 collaboration with American-born experimental guitarist Henry Kaiser. Two other volumes soon followed, with volume 2 being nominated for a Grammy award. Today he remains extremely popular and is still producing albums, including the 2011 *Mitapolaka*.

In the towns, posters invite local residents to jazz concerts—or to a spectacular fashion show that will attract men and women alike. The most successful local groups playing pop music in Malagasy style have been Mahaleo and Tarika Sammy (who made it to the international music world along with other artists like Jaojoby, Rajery, and accordionist Regis Gizavo). Other well-known contemporary pop groups and singers include Tearano, Freddy de Majunga, Tiana, Dama, and Rebika. There are occasional classical music concerts as well.

ARCHITECTURE

Building styles depend on the materials available. Brick and corrugated iron are used on the high plateau where there are hardly any trees left for timber. Coastal homes may have a framework of wooden poles, with walls and roof made of palm fronds, thatch, woven matting, or mud and wattle (interwoven reeds and thin poles). Where there is suitable wood, the Malagasy enjoy carving patterned posts or face-boards for verandas and porches.

The compass points of a house are important, and each direction has its own significance. For example, the north represents power and the south suggests bad influences. According to the Malagasy cosmological system, the north axis is superior to the south, and the east axis is superior to the west. Malagasy houses are always oriented on the north-south axis, as that is believed to correspond to the world of the living. Guests are to be seated in the north or northwest of the house, while the northeast corner is sacred to the ancestors, holding objects of ceremonial use. In the south part of the house may be the hearth, in a square pit, with cooking pots, ax, and firewood set against the wall. The east is considered sacred. The husband's bed is thus usually beside the east wall, where he sleeps with his head to the north.

In the cities, houses are built mostly of red brick, but some blocks of plastered concrete are painted cream, green, or off-white. Antananarivo has some gracious buildings dating from French colonial days; these have tall windows, wrought-iron balconies, and shutters. Middle-income homes have two or three stories, often with the kitchen at the top, living quarters in the middle, and storage space below. Most town houses have wide balconies supported by brick columns and are crowned with steep, tiled roofs.

CRAFTS

There is an obvious distinction between articles made of recycled modern scrap and articles made of natural materials with a long tradition of design behind them, yet the Malagasy have become very ingenious at recycling castoffs. Discarded tomato puree cans are made into oil lamps, and soft drink cans become brightly colored model cars. Watering cans are made from milk-powder cans, and wire is used to create egg baskets or environmentally friendly mousetraps that catch the mouse alive, to be eaten or set free elsewhere. French-style, long-handled garden spades are made from bits of old cars. Discarded tires are turned into sandals. Raffia is woven into market baskets with leather handles or hats with wide brims. Rugs are made from raffia and rags.

True craftsmen carve in wood and horn. Wood carving from Ambositra is famous, as is the furniture made in Betsileo of valuable hardwoods. The objects created are most often practical and include headrests, stools, and walking sticks. Tourists buy boxes with inlaid designs, model sailboats, chess

Spread among some one hundred tiny villages, the Zafimaniry people live in the forested mountains of Madagascar's southern Central Highlands. The people, who number about 25,000, are known for being the last remaining artisans of a unique woodcraft culture that was once widespread on the island.

The United Nations Educational, Scientific and Cultural Organization (UNESCO) recognizes this specialized knowledge as an "Intangible Cultural Heritage of Humanity." UNESCO defines this as "the practices, representations, expressions, knowledge, skills—as well as the [associated] instruments, objects, artefacts and cultural spaces—that [a people] recognize as part of their cultural heritage." The Zafimaniry's woodcraft knowledge is Madagascar's sole cultural heritage listed by UNESCO.

The carpenters embellish practically all the wooden surfaces of their houses and objects with elaborate ornamentation, and their homes and other structures are expertly fitted together without nails or metal hardware of any kind. The patterns reflect not only the community's Austronesian origins but Arab influences as well, and have rich symbolic significance. A tanamparoratra *(spider's web), for example, symbolizes family ties, while a* papintantely *(honeycomb) represents community life. The designs can also indicate a person's role and social standing within the community.*

sets made from semiprecious stones, and solitaire, a one-player board game played with thirty-two pegs or counters. The goal is to jump over the pegs horizontally or vertically until there is only one peg left on the board. The beauty of almost anything in Madagascar is determined by its usefulness.

In the town of Antaimoro, a decorative papyrus-like paper, with dried flowers embedded in it, is used to make wall hangings and lampshades. It

A woman sells colorful fabrics in Antsiranana while caring for her daughter.

was originally produced from the pulped bark of the avoha tree, but now sisal is used as well.

Women enjoy wearing lambas made from locally produced cotton or silk colored with herbal dyes. The silk is woven from fibers produced by silkworms raised on mulberry or tapia leaves. Particularly attractive is the *lambahoany* (LAM-ba-OON), the colorful cloth of the widespread Sakalava group. Ornamental cloth is made of finely woven raffia, and decorative tablecloths and mats are crocheted or embroidered.

Market vendors do not have set prices for their goods, so all transactions involve a fair bit of bargaining. Much of the craftwork on sale is intended for tourists, but the Malagasy like to decorate their houses as well. A serious attempt is being made to stop the production and sale of items originating from endangered creatures, such as tortoise shell, snakeskin, coral, and stuffed lemurs.

TEXTILES

Weaving is popular in Madagascar and has distinct features not found anywhere else within the African context. Silk, cotton, wool, raffia, and bast fibers are used alone or in combinations on the many types of looms found on the island. Malagasy weaving technology appears to reflect the mixture of Malayo-Polynesian, African, and Arab influences that is also evident in the peoples' cultures. In Madagascar, only women weave.

The Merina loom, similar in style to those found in Southeast Asia, does not rely on a fixed structure of weight to create the required tension; instead, it uses the weight of the weaver's body.

Most cloth is woven in stripes of different widths and colors. It can have a border decorated with small silver beads. Silk weaving comes mostly from the Merina and Betsileo people; cotton, once widespread, is now mainly from Betsileo; wool is associated with the south; bast fiber with Merina, Tanala, and Betsileo; and raffia, the fiber most widely used, with Betsimisaraka, Sakalava, Merina, and Tanala.

The warp-striped lamba cloth used to be worn by everyone and removed only when some vigorous task had to be undertaken. Distinct from this common wrap is the *lamba mena*, the shroud reserved for wrapping dead bodies. The earliest records indicate that these were always woven of silk and dyed red. Now the color red is not always predominant and a shroud may contain colors prescribed by the *ombiasy*, who determines the most favorable colors for a particular ancestor.

In recent years, Madagascar's textile art has seen a revival of sorts with famous fashion houses such as Yves Saint Laurent using local handwoven fabrics in their creations. In Antananarivo, local fabrics dominate fashion runways. Increasingly, affluent Malagasy wear Western-inspired vests, ties, handbags, and hats made of these beautiful textiles.

INTERNET LINKS

https://ich.unesco.org/en/RL/woodcrafting-knowledge-of-the-zafimaniry-00080
The Intangible Cultural Heritage page for the woodcrafting of the Zafimaniry includes slides.

https://www.musicinafrica.net/magazine/traditional-music-madagascar
This site offers a good overview of Madagascar's traditional music.

https://www.rom.on.ca/en/collections-research/research-community-projects/world-culture/in-living-colour-the-roms-unique
This museum site provides good historic information and many photos of Malagasy textile arts.

LEISURE

Young boys play soccer with a homemade ball and bare feet.

AS IN MANY OTHER COUNTRIES, Malagasy children seem always to be kicking a soccer ball around or playing a makeshift game of baseball or cricket in many districts across Madagascar. In schools, games such as soccer, volleyball, basketball, boxing, and tennis are primarily played as organized sports.

ENTHUSIASM FOR SPORTS

Athletics are popular, with interregional school meets as well as professional participation in the All-Africa Games. Students compete at soccer using a local stadium in the mornings, with smartly dressed teams, uniformed referees, and linesmen. In the evenings and on the weekends, their fathers take over the stadiums for the adult games. Madagascar has a national soccer team nicknamed the Barea (named for a species of zebu that is also on the country's coat of arms), but the team has never qualified for the finals in the World Cup or the African Nations Cup tournaments. Newspapers keep readers up to date with news of local and world soccer stars. During the World Cup soccer seasons, many cafés display tablecloths featuring the top teams. Girls as well as boys play the game.

There is also enthusiasm for tennis, although it is an expensive sport to organize. Malagasy athletes excel in tennis, participating in both the Fed Cup (a competition in women's tennis) and the Davis Cup (a

A tourist paddles a small canoe on the Tsiribihina River.

competition for men's tennis). Two sisters in particular, Dally and Natacha Randriantefy, were high-achieving athletes in this sport, with Dally, who retired in 2006, winning Madagascar's first gold medal in the All-Africa Games in Harare in 1995.

Cycling is popular, and tourists have discovered that the rough trails and country roads are ideal for scenic mountain biking. They also enjoy organized canoe trips on the rivers Tsiribihina and Manambaho in the west. Whale watching is fast gaining in popularity, especially around Maroantsetra and off the coast of Nosy Boraha. Tennis courts, swimming pools, and golf clubs in Antananarivo and some other major centers are legacies of French colonial occupation. A relatively new sport is horse racing, with interest and support from South Africa. Newspapers in Antananarivo carry details of handball league championships and table tennis competitions.

Madagascar first participated in the Olympic Games in 1964 and has sent outstanding athletes to subsequent Olympics, but has yet to take home any medals.

LOCAL SPORTS

If in the more traditional areas of Madagascar people seem to show little interest in organized Western-style sports, it does not mean they do not like to show off their athletic prowess and bravery. There are several indigenous sports events. In the highlands south of Antananarivo, in the cattle country of Ambositra, there is a form of bullfighting known as *tolon'omby* (to-lon-OMB) that resembles an American rodeo. Young men dash among bulls that are inside a stockade, trying to catch one by the horns (or hump or tail) and hold on as long as possible. The crowd roars its approval at displays of bravery and skill or jeers if the youth falls too quickly.

The Sakalava have a style of martial arts called *moraingy* (mor-AIN-gi) where two opponents swing blows at each other with arms and bare fists until one steps back. The fighting is fast and tough, with emphasis on agility. The objective is to knock one's opponent flat on his back.

As might be expected from a population closely linked to Indonesia and the East, oriental martial arts are popular, although there are uneasy memories of the 1985 street violence in Antananarivo attributed to the kung fu clubs there.

A Betsileo man fights a Zebu bull during a traditional zebu bullfight. Unlike in Spanish bullfighting, the animal is neither tortured nor killed in this sport.

Boys play with an old table soccer game.

GAMES

The board game *fanorona* (fan-or-OON), a complicated Malagasy version of checkers, is a national pastime. A complex grid of crisscrossed lines is marked out on the ground (or on specially made stone blocks in public arcades) and two opponents move counters, encouraged by a crowd. Each player tries to "eat" his opponent's pieces. It is a leisurely game that does not require speed, for there are traps everywhere. The philosophy of fanorona rests in the idea that life presents many possibilities. The outcome prized most by experienced players is a tie or becoming deadlocked, for the goal is not direct aggression but to stop one's opponent from moving. There is even a national fanorona organization.

Another game is *katra* (KAH-trr), a mancala game that involves shifting piles of stones around a board until one player has won all the stones.

The café version of football, foosball, with rows of wooden players on little metal rods, is highly popular with young men. They play pool or table tennis as well. The departure lounge of a small-town airport is sometimes used as a social club in the evenings. Men gather there for a beer or to play cards or dominoes.

Young children play hopscotch, scratching an eight-square pattern in the dust and hopping on one foot, while kicking a piece of wood onto the next square. Older kids listen to imported music on cassettes or twist happily at the local dance clubs. Antananarivo has about a dozen dance clubs, and most towns have at least one.

POPULAR MEDIA

The government-controlled Malagasy Broadcasting System broadcasts television as well as radio programs in Malagasy and French. On most days television viewing starts at noon and includes cartoons, sports programs, news in French and Malagasy, and films from France and the United States. There are also two private TV stations. However, not many homes have television—only about 39 percent of households, as of 2010.

There are few movie theaters apart from those in Antananarivo and the larger towns. In the capital city, the Albert Camus Cultural Center has theater programs and concerts, varying from classical to jazz and rock. Films are shown at the Alliance Française centers (found in many towns) and at several embassies in Antananarivo.

INTERNET LINKS

http://www.bbc.com/news/world-africa-13861846
The BBC provides a quick overview of media in Madagascar.

FESTIVALS

A Malagasy Father Christmas visits the children of Ambohibary on Christmas Day.

12

ALTHOUGH THERE ARE RELIGIOUS and political festivals developed from colonial influence and contact with the Western world, old cultural festivals connected with the natural cycles of the year are also celebrated in Madagascar. In some places, for example, a Festival of Trees or Festival of Rice is held in April or May to celebrate the harvest.

This appeals to people in the rural areas, where the preparation, growth, and harvesting of rice mark the progress of time far more memorably than any public holiday. A successful rice harvest ensures survival, so it is hardly surprising that common expressions concerning time refer to how long it takes to cook a pot of rice or the time it takes for rice seedlings to sprout.

Other holidays mark religious or political events. If a holiday falls on a Thursday, it is extended to Friday to create a longer weekend.

The Catholic and Protestant churches observe religious festivals with worship services in much the same way as anywhere else in the world. The Malagasy have adopted from the French Catholics their love of incense, processions, and ceremonial rituals. They observe Christmas and Easter, the main Christian festivals, in conventional style. Father Christmas is known as le Bonhomme Noël in French or Dadabenoely in Malagasy and is portrayed in the usual red outfit trimmed with white fur despite the heat of a tropical summer in December. The small Muslim

At Christmastime, this poem is very popular with Malagasy children: *Krismasy re no tonga* (Christmas is coming) *Falifaly ny kilonga* (Children are happy) *Krismasy tena fety* (Christmas is a feast) *Ho an'ny kely sy vaventy* (For young and old).

minority celebrates Eid al-Fitr to mark the end of the month of fasting during Ramadan. Gifts will be given to children who fast for the first time or have completed their entire month of fasting.

POLITICAL HOLIDAYS

On March 29 (Martyrs' Day) people remember the 1947 rebellion led by Joseph Raseta and Joseph Ravoahangy against French domination. The insurrection was crushed and thousands of Malagasy were killed: some estimates say as many as eighty thousand peoplpe perished. Nevertheless, it was the beginning of a popular movement that eventually led to the country's longed-for independence in 1960.

This event is celebrated as Independence Day on June 26. There is a weeklong program of patriotic events leading to the day, when schoolchildren parade with banners proclaiming the republic's motto, "Fatherland, Liberty, Progress." They sing the national anthem and watch the national flag being raised. Speeches, singing, and processions follow, and there is usually a Grand Ball and family feasting in the evening. The Anniversary of the Democratic Republic of Madagascar (or Republic Day) is recognized in similar style on December 30.

Fireworks commemorate Independence Day, June 26, on the shores of Lake Anosy in the nation's capital.

OFFICIAL PUBLIC HOLIDAYS

January 1	New Year's Day
March 29	Martyrs' Day
April*	Good Friday, Easter Sunday and Monday
May 1	Workers' Day (Labor Day)
May 25	Organization of African Unity Day
May*	Ascension Day
May*	Pentecost Monday
June 26	Independence Day
August 15	Assumption Day
November 1	All Saints' Day
December 25	Christmas Day
December 30	Republic Day, or Anniversary of the Democratic Republic of Madagascar

The exact dates vary from year to year.

The internationally observed Labor Day on May 1 was instituted when Communist ideals were being enforced during the presidency of Didier Ratsiraka, but it is now observed as Workers' Day by the present trade unions.

Madagascar is a member of the African Union (AU) and a member of the United Nations, so May 25, which is the Organization of African Unity Day, is an opportunity to spotlight the country's political links with the African mainland. The Malagasy do not consider themselves to be Africans, but because of the legacy of French colonial rule, the island has developed political, economic, and cultural ties to the French-speaking countries of western Africa. It is also regarded as advantageous to have friendly trade links with the mainland.

TRADITIONAL FESTIVITIES

The New Year is Madagascar's most popular festival and a time for gift giving. Also celebrated is *Alahamady Be*, or the first new moon in the first month of the Malagasy New Year.

The *famadihana* ceremony of reburial should be undertaken every year for one or more ancestors, but few families can afford this. By law, this ritual must take place between June and September, presumably because they are the cooler months and the opening of a tomb will present less of a health hazard in terms of unpleasant odors and disease.

Circumcision is practiced in Madagascar as a fertility rite. It is performed on boys generally between five and six years old, also mostly during June to September, as these dry, cool months help in the healing of the wound from circumcision. Circumcision is not regarded as the rite of passage between adolescence and adulthood as it is in many parts of the African mainland. Among the Antaimoro people in the southeast, the ceremony is observed only once every seven years and the feast may go on for several days. There are specific fady rules: uncircumcised boys are not "men" and may not marry, nor be laid in the family tomb. While still uncircumcised, boys must not handle sharp iron instruments.

Another celebrated occasion is when a baby's hair is cut for the first time. Among the Antambahoka in the south, the baby's grandparents will do the honor of cutting the hair. For the Merina people, only a man whose parents are still alive is allowed to perform the ritual. The baby is then put in a basin filled with water and bathed. Afterward, the family will have a meal of rice, zebu meat, milk, and honey.

MUSIC FESTIVALS

Donia is a traditional music festival held at Nosy Be in the month of May or June. Scores of musicians from parts of Madagascar, Mauritius, Réunion, and Seychelles enliven this four-day annual event, which also features sports events and a carnival. In November or December, Antananarivo hosts the

Gasytsara Modern Music Festival. And Madajazzcar, a week-long jazz festival that began in 1988, kicks off on the first Saturday of October. This fest attracts performers from all over the world and is regarded as one of Africa's most important jazz events.

Folk musicians and dancers entertain in December in the fishing village of Ramena.

INTERNET LINKS

http://www.iexplore.com/articles/travel-guides/africa/madagascar/festivals-and-events
Traditional festivals as well as the usual public holidays are listed on this site.

http://www.madajazzcar.mg
This is the home site of the Madajazzcar music festival, which can be translated from French to English.

https://www.timeanddate.com/holidays/madagascar
This site lists the dates for public holidays in Madagascar by year.

FOOD

A young woman offers rice at a market in Belo-sur-Tsiribhine.

13

THE FOODS OF MADAGASCAR reflect the island's geographical setting as well as its history. The culinary traditions of the French, Chinese, Indian—and to a lesser degree, East African and Arabian—cultures are represented in the island's cuisine. Rice is a staple that is served at most every meal.

At home, most Malagasy eat by sitting on a mat on the floor. All the food is laid out at the same time, and large spoons are used to scoop food from common dishes. Tradition requires that the oldest member of the family eats and drinks first but should always stop eating before the young are served to make sure there will be enough food for them.

RICE

The Malagasy eat about a pound (half a kilogram) of rice, which they call *vary* (VAR), daily and consider themselves poorly treated if it is not available. For variety, they cook it differently for each meal. At breakfast, the rice may be watery (like a rice porridge), or eaten dry and sprinkled with sugar or with any available sliced fruit. For lunch and dinner, it is eaten dry and served with onion or another vegetable. In well-to-do households, French bread spread with butter replaces rice as breakfast food.

A Malagasy cook does not decide whether or not to have rice, but merely chooses what to have with it, using what is locally available

The popularity of rice in the Malagasy diet reflects the people's ancient South Asian ancestry. In the Malagasy language, "to eat a meal"–*mihinam-bary*–literally means "to eat rice."

Farm workers prepare the rice harvest.

and in season. Everything goes with rice—perhaps a boiled or fried egg, or a few bits of stewed or boiled zebu beef, fish, chicken, or duck. Popular side dishes to go with rice are peas flavored with pork, whitefish with zucchini and tomato, beans in tomato sauce, and pumpkin-peanut puree. With this may come a small bowl of *ranovola* (RAHN-o-VOOL), which is water boiled with the residue in the rice pot, or *brêdes* (BREED), which is boiled greens, to finish off the meal.

Rice is not only a substantial staple food, it is also a prominent feature of Malagasy culture. Growing rice requires more people than one household can provide, so families have to help one another. They join together to trample the ground to prepare it for the planting of seeds, take turns in "rice watching"—making sure that the birds do not eat the sown seed and that cattle or wild pigs do not trample the young plants—and then harvest the crop. Even pounding the rice with a heavy wooden pestle can be turned into a sort of dancing game in which a circle of four to six women throw the pestle across to one another while keeping up a steady rhythm.

FAVORITE FOODS

The national meat dish is *romazava* (room-a-ZAHV), a beef and vegetable stew in thin gravy with tomato, onion, and a hint of ginger. It is served with rice, greens, and perhaps a salad. Another favorite is *ravitoto* (RAH-vee-TOOT-o), which is made of shredded cassava leaves with peanuts or fried pork. Red meats such as beef are a luxury, so small mammals often end up in the cooking pot. Villagers usually eat beef only occasionally, perhaps after a rare ceremonial slaughter of one of their precious zebu.

Their cooking is seldom strongly spiced; instead, commonly used ingredients like garlic, onion, ginger, tomato, mild curry, and salt are used to flavor their dishes. In the coastal areas, the use of coconut milk, vanilla, and

A plate of ravitoto, a traditional dish made of pounded cassava leaves, garlic, and pork or zebu, is served with rice at a restaurant.

A bounty of typical Malagasy dishes is arrayed on a wooden table.

spices such as cloves are popular. The Malagasy also enjoy mouth-searing sauces, though, such as the Indian-style condiment made of pickled mango, lemon, and other fruits. Usually eaten along the coast, this condiment is growing in popularity among many Malagasy highlanders. Other hot sauces include a fiery pepper sauce, and *rougaille* (roo-GUY), made from tomatoes, ginger, onions, lemon, and hot peppers.

They bake their bread, *mofo* (MOOF), in long thin loaves like French baguettes. In many villages, cassava or manioc root (which looks like a yam but has its own taste) is used as a bread substitute.

Chicken, *akoho*, is on the menu in many variations and so is turkey, a bird not restricted by any local *fady*. Only gray-haired people may raise, though not eat, geese, since they have the gray hair that dispels the *fady* of the gray geese. Coastal fishers add crab, crayfish, shrimp, prawns, oysters, and many varieties of fish to their menu, although most of the catch is sold to hotels and restaurants rather than eaten at home.

EATING OUT

Going to a *hotely*, or restaurant, is an indulgence for the rich only. A lunchtime excursion is not as popular as an evening one because of the midday heat. In the evening, after a drink perhaps on an open veranda, dinner may last from 7 p.m. until late at night. The menu might include paella, a mound of seasoned rice surrounded by shrimp, pieces of chicken, hunks of crab, and lobster claws with a tomato, onion, and shrimp sauce. Vegetarian dishes are limited in many areas of Madagascar, and bean dishes are not as common as

in mainland Africa. Some Indian restaurants in Antananarivo and Mahajanga, however, do serve vegetarian food.

The influence of their ancestral lands is found in the popularity of Chinese and Indian restaurants. They have adapted the noodle-rich Chinese soup into a most filling meal, with greens and bits of seafood or chicken in a broth prepared with coriander and served with a sprinkling of soy sauce.

Those who prefer a less expensive meal will find it at a *gargotte*, or roadside stall. On street corners, rows of vendors offer snacks in abundance. Most common is *mofo gasy* (MOOF gash), Malagasy bread made from a batter of sweetened rice flour and cooked over greased circular molds. This is a popular breakfast item, often enjoyed with a cup of coffee. There are many varieties of bread, one of which is made with chopped greens, tomatoes, and peppers. Other street snacks include deep-fried corn-flour donuts, rice pudding, and homemade yogurt.

A small roadside stand sells *mofo gasy* along the highlands highway in central Madagascar.

The fruits of the screwpine, which is not a pine but a palmlike pandanus plant, may be juiced or used for their seeds.

SWEETS

Dessert in Madagascar is usually fruit. From October to December there are fresh pineapples, lychees, strawberries, mangoes, guavas, and bananas growing wild that can be picked and eaten on the spot. In the markets, oranges, peaches, pears, apricots, and apples are available. Coconut is eaten in fresh slices, drunk (as water from the nut), or cooked into sweets. The Malagasy serve bananas in many ways: fried in batter, cooked inside a pancake, or flamed in rum, which can be considered the national dessert.

Nibblers buy slices of *parique* (pa-REEK), made from peanuts, rice, and sugar, and wrapped and baked in banana leaves. There is a local dark chocolate with a bitter flavor, and peanut brittle or loose peanuts are always available.

Malagasy cheeses are made almost exclusively in the south central highlands, including a delicious pepper cheese. Zebu cattle provide little milk, so there are few other dairy products.

DRINKS

Although the poor have no choice, the water that comes out of the communal taps is seldom safe to drink by Western standards. The common beverage is *ranovola*, rice water, which is water boiled in an almost-empty rice pot, flavored by leftover grains of burned rice (boiling makes it safer to drink than water from the tap or river). It is strained and served cold. Fresh milk is not easily available, so the Malagasy drink their coffee or tea without milk, providing sticky condensed milk for tourists who require it.

Coconut milk, made from the white meat of the coconut, is a popular drink in the coastal towns: mixed with rum it becomes *punch aux cocos* (PAHN-ch aw KO-ko). There are several varieties of commercially distilled rum, often with added vanilla, honey, or lemongrass flavors. Variations of crude alcohol made from rice, sugarcane, coconut, or lychees are made for local consumption. The national beer is a lager named Three Horses, which is ironic since horses are a rarity on Madagascar.

Small vineyards, mostly around Ambalavao and Fianarantsoa, produce fruity local wines such as Domremy, d'Antsirabe, Betsileo, and Côte de Fianer.

Tourists drink coconut water straight from the fruit itself.

INTERNET LINKS

https://afktravel.com/97288/incredible-edibles-10-foods-from-madagascar-that-you-have-to-try
This slideshow of Malagasy specialties provides a quick look at the cuisine.

http://www.foodandwine.com/articles/flavors-of-madagascar
This article discusses five seasonings from Madagascar that changed the world.

AKOHO SY VOANIO (MADAGASCAR CHICKEN IN COCONUT MILK)

This is one of the most popular main courses on the island.

2 Tablespoons oil
1 onion, thinly sliced
3 garlic cloves, finely chopped
2 Tbsp fresh ginger, grated
2 cups (475 mL) coconut milk
1 vanilla bean, split
¼ teaspoon ground cloves
½ tsp ground turmeric
1 Tbsp curry powder
1 cup (240 mL) chicken
   broth or water
1.5 lb (680 g) chicken thighs
   (boneless and skinless), cut
   into chunks
2 plum tomatoes, chopped
Salt, pepper

Heat oil in a deep frying pan or Dutch oven. Add onion, garlic, and ginger. Sauté over medium-low heat for about 1 minute.

Add coconut milk, vanilla bean, and spices. Add the chicken broth or water and bring to a boil.

Add chicken pieces. Reduce to a simmer and cook for 20 minutes, until chicken is cooked through.

Add tomato, salt and black pepper to taste. Simmer another 5 minutes. Serve with rice.

GODRO-GODRO

This sweet is a firm, cake-like coconut milk pudding.

2 cups (400 g) sugar, separated into halves
½ cup (120 mL) water
2 13-ounce cans (800 mL) coconut milk
1 tsp vanilla extract
¾ tsp ground cinnamon
¾ tsp ground nutmeg
¼ tsp ground cloves
5 Tbsp + 3 Tbsp oil
4 cups (950 mL) water
3 cups (360 g) wheat semolina (cream of wheat)

In a small heavy saucepan, combine 1 cup (200 g) sugar and ½ cup (120 mL) water. Heat on medium-high, stirring constantly, until sugar crystals dissolve and the liquid boils. Let cook without stirring, swirling the pot occasionally, until sugar is golden brown (caramelized). Remove from heat immediately.

In a large pot, heat coconut milk to boiling, then reduce heat to medium. Pour liquid caramel into coconut milk slowly, stirring constantly to prevent liquid from boiling over, until both liquids are well blended. Add vanilla, spices, 5 Tbsp oil, remaining water, and semolina. Whisk until batter becomes very thick. Stir with a large spoon until the mix forms a solid mass that cleans the sides of the pot. Pour into a well greased 13-inch x 8-inch (33 x 20 cm) baking dish (or a round cake pan) and spread evenly. Next, drizzle 3 Tbsp oil on top.

Preheat oven to 400°F (200°C). Make another batch of caramel using 1 cup (200 g) sugar and ½ cup (120 mL) water, using the same method as before. Pour caramel over the cake and spread quickly before the caramel hardens. Bake the cake for 20 minutes. Chill before serving, preferably overnight in the refrigerator.

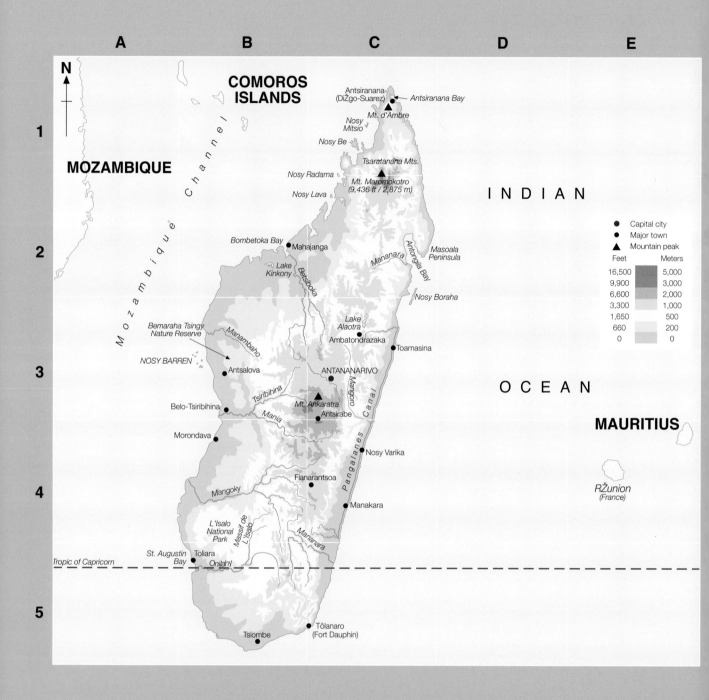

N

A B C D E

COMOROS
ISLANDS

MOZAMBIQUE

Antsiranana
(DiŽgo-Suarez) ● ← Antsiranana Bay
▲ Mt. d'Ambre
Nosy
Mitsio

Nosy Be

Nosy Radama   Tsaratanana Mts.
                ▲
Nosy Lava   Mt. Maromokotro
                (9,436 ft / 2,875 m)

INDIAN

● Capital city
● Major town
▲ Mountain peak

Feet	Meters
16,500	5,000
9,900	3,000
6,600	2,000
3,300	1,000
1,650	500
660	200
0	0

Bombetoka Bay ● Mahajanga

Lake
Kinkony

Betsiboka

Mananara

Masoala
Peninsula

Antongila Bay

Nosy Boraha

Bemaraha Tsingy
Nature Reserve

NOSY BARREN

Manambaho

Lake
Alaotra

Antsalova ●

Ambatondrazaka ●

ANTANANARIVO ●

Toamasina ●

OCEAN

MAURITIUS

Belo-Tsiribihina ●

Tsiribihina

Mania

Mt. Ankaratra ▲
Antsirabe ●

Mangoro Canal

Pangalanes Canal

Morondava ●

Nosy Varika ●

Fianarantsoa ●

Mangoky

Manakara ●

L'Isalo
National
Park

Massif de L'Isalo

Mananara

RŽunion
(France)

Tropic of Capricorn

St. Augustin Toliara ●
Bay
Onilahy

Tsiombe ●

Tôlanaro ●
(Fort Dauphin)

MAP OF MADAGASCAR

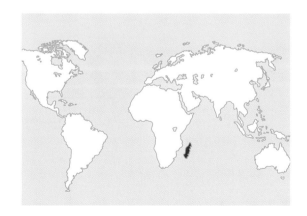

ECONOMIC MADAGASCAR

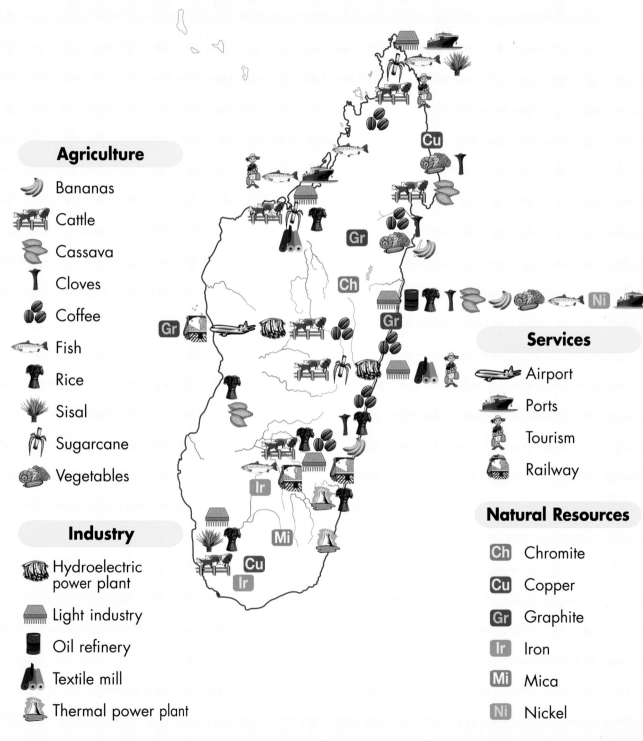

Agriculture

- Bananas
- Cattle
- Cassava
- Cloves
- Coffee
- Fish
- Rice
- Sisal
- Sugarcane
- Vegetables

Industry

- Hydroelectric power plant
- Light industry
- Oil refinery
- Textile mill
- Thermal power plant

Services

- Airport
- Ports
- Tourism
- Railway

Natural Resources

- Ch Chromite
- Cu Copper
- Gr Graphite
- Ir Iron
- Mi Mica
- Ni Nickel

ABOUT THE ECONOMY

TYPE OF ECONOMY
free market

GROSS DOMESTIC PRODUCT (GDP)
(official exchange rate)
$9.74 billion (2016)

GDP GROWTH RATE
4.1 percent (2016)

INFLATION RATE
6.7 percent (2016)

WORKFORCE
12.98 million (2016)

UNEMPLOYMENT RATE
3.6 percent (2014)

POPULATION BELOW POVERTY LINE
70.7 percent (2012)

CURRENCY
1 Malagasy ariary (MGA) = 5 iraimbilanja
Notes: 10,000, 5,000, 1,000, 500, 200, 100 ariary
Coins: 50, 20, 10, 5, 4, 2, 1 ariary; 2, 1 iraimbilanja
1 USD = 2937.50 MGA (August 2017)

NATURAL RESOURCES
graphite, chromite, coal, bauxite, rare earth elements, salt, quartz, tar sands, semiprecious stones, mica, fish, hydropower

AGRICULTURAL PRODUCTS
Coffee, vanilla, sugarcane, cloves, cocoa, rice, cassava, beans, bananas, peanuts, livestock products

INDUSTRIES
meat processing, seafood, soap, beer, leather, sugar, textiles, glassware, cement, automobile assembly plant, paper, petroleum, tourism, mining

EXPORTS
Coffee, vanilla, shellfish, sugar, cotton cloth, clothing, chromite, and petroleum products

IMPORTS
Capital goods (production equipment like machinery that is used to produce other goods), petroleum, foodstuffs, consumer goods (goods for personal use such as food, medicine, and clothing)

EXPORT PARTNERS
France, United States, China, South Africa, Japan, Netherland, India, Germany, Belgium (2015)

IMPORT PARTNERS
China, France, Bahrain, India, Kuwait, Mauritius, South Africa (2015)

LAND USE
Agricultural land, 71.1 percent; forest, 21.5 percent; other, 7.4 percent (2011)

CULTURAL MADAGASCAR

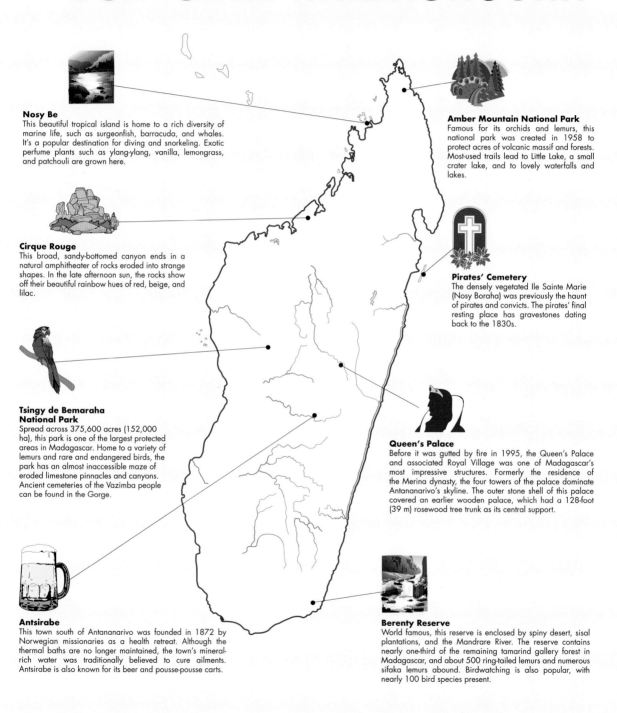

Nosy Be
This beautiful tropical island is home to a rich diversity of marine life, such as surgeonfish, barracuda, and whales. It's a popular destination for diving and snorkeling. Exotic perfume plants such as ylang-ylang, vanilla, lemongrass, and patchouli are grown here.

Cirque Rouge
This broad, sandy-bottomed canyon ends in a natural amphitheater of rocks eroded into strange shapes. In the late afternoon sun, the rocks show off their beautiful rainbow hues of red, beige, and lilac.

Tsingy de Bemaraha National Park
Spread across 375,600 acres (152,000 ha), this park is one of the largest protected areas in Madagascar. Home to a variety of lemurs and rare and endangered birds, the park has an almost inaccessible maze of eroded limestone pinnacles and canyons. Ancient cemeteries of the Vazimba people can be found in the Gorge.

Antsirabe
This town south of Antananarivo was founded in 1872 by Norwegian missionaries as a health retreat. Although the thermal baths are no longer maintained, the town's mineral-rich water was traditionally believed to cure ailments. Antsirabe is also known for its beer and pousse-pousse carts.

Amber Mountain National Park
Famous for its orchids and lemurs, this national park was created in 1958 to protect acres of volcanic massif and forests. Most-used trails lead to Little Lake, a small crater lake, and to lovely waterfalls and lakes.

Pirates' Cemetery
The densely vegetated Ile Sainte Marie (Nosy Boraha) was previously the haunt of pirates and convicts. The pirates' final resting place has gravestones dating back to the 1830s.

Queen's Palace
Before it was gutted by fire in 1995, the Queen's Palace and associated Royal Village was one of Madagascar's most impressive structures. Formerly the residence of the Merina dynasty, the four towers of the palace dominate Antananarivo's skyline. The outer stone shell of this palace covered an earlier wooden palace, which had a 128-foot (39 m) rosewood tree trunk as its central support.

Berenty Reserve
World famous, this reserve is enclosed by spiny desert, sisal plantations, and the Mandrare River. The reserve contains nearly one-third of the remaining tamarind gallery forest in Madagascar, and about 500 ring-tailed lemurs and numerous sifaka lemurs abound. Birdwatching is also popular, with nearly 100 bird species present.

ABOUT THE CULTURE

OFFICIAL NAME
Repoblikan'i Madagasikara (Republic of Madagascar)

FLAG DESCRIPTION
Two equal horizontal bands of red (top half) and green with a vertical white band of the same width on the hoist side.

TOTAL AREA
226,657 square miles (587,042 square km); land: 224,533 square miles (581,540 square km); water: 2,124 square miles (5,500 square km)

CAPITAL
Antananarivo

POPULATION
25,054,161 (2017)

ETHNIC GROUPS
Malayo-Indonesian (Merina and related Betsileo), Côtiers (mixed African, Malayo-Indonesian, and Arab ancestry— Betsimisaraka, Tsimihety, Antaisaka, Sakalava), French, Indian, Creole, Comorian

LANGUAGES
Malagasy (official), French (official), English

RELIGIOUS GROUPS
Indigenous religionist, Christian, Muslim

BIRTHRATE
31.6 births/1,000 population (2017)

DEATH RATE
6.5 deaths/1,000 population (2017)

INFANT MORTALITY RATE
42.4 deaths/1,000 live births (2016)

LIFE EXPECTANCY AT BIRTH
Total population: 65.9 years
Male: 64.4 years
Female: 67.4 years (2016)

LITERACY
64.7 percent (2015)

TIMELINE

IN MADAGASCAR	IN THE WORLD

ca. 1 CE
Madagascar is settled by Malayo-Polynesians.

1100
Rise of the Incan civilization in Peru

1500
The Portuguese discover Madagascar, naming it the Isle of Saint Lawrence.

1492
Christopher Columbus sails to the Americas.

1650s
The kingdom of Sakalava on the western coast emerges.

1558–1603
Reign of Elizabeth I of England

1716
The Betsimisaraka empire emerges under Ratsimilaho, the son of an English pirate and a Malagasy princess.

1810–1828
Reign of Radama I, a Merina king. British missionaries convert the court to Christianity. Merina culture begins to spread.

1789–1799
The French Revolution

1861–1863
Reign of Radama II

1861–1865
American Civil War

1869
The Suez Canal is opened.

1883–1885
The Franco-Malagasy War. Madagascar signs peace treaty giving France greater influence in Malagasy affairs.

1896
France annexes Madagascar.

1897
The Merina queen is exiled, and Madagascar becomes a French protectorate.

1914–1919
World War I

1939–1945
World War II

1946
Madagascar becomes an Overseas Territory of France.

1947
French Army crushes a Merina insurrection—80,000 are killed.

IN MADAGASCAR	IN THE WORLD

1958
Madagascar votes for autonomy.

1960
Madagascar gains independence with Philibert Tsiranana as the first president.

1972
Tsiranana dissolves parliament,; hands power to Gabriel Ramanantsoa.

1975
Admiral Didier Ratsiraka stages a coup and rules for most of next 30 years.

1969
Neil Armstrong becomes the first human to walk on the moon.

1986
Nuclear power disaster at Chernobyl in Ukraine

1991
Breakup of the Soviet Union

2001
Marc Ravalomanana claims victory after disputed presidential election. Ratsiraka flees.

2001
Terrorists crash planes in New York, Washington DC, and Pennsylvania.

2003
War in Iraq begins.

2008
Cyclone Ivan kills 93 people.

2008
US elects first African American president, Barack Obama.

2009–2010
Political crisis. Violent protests; Andry Rajoelina assumes power in coup; President Ravalomanana flees; is sentenced to prison. Voters endorse new constitution.

2014
Hery Rajaonarimampianina wins election, becomes president, restores democratic rule.

2015
Senate is elected after being dissolved in 2009.

2015–2016
ISIS launches terror attacks in Belgium and France.

2016
Three years of severe drought in southern Madagascar causes extreme hunger.

2017
Cyclone Enawo, strongest storm in 13 years, hits north of Madagascar.

2017
Donald Trump becomes US president.
Britain begins Brexit process of leaving the EU.

GLOSSARY

Alahamady Be
First new moon in first month of the Malagasy New Year.

côtiers (COH-ti-ay)
Coastal people.

Eid al-Fitr
Muslim celebration to mark the end of Ramadan, a month of obligatory fasting.

fady (FAH-di)
Forbidden, taboo.

fanorona (fan-or-OON)
Malagasy board game.

fokontany (FOOK-on-TAN)
Localized community rule.

haiteny (HAY-ten-i)
Traditional style of love poetry.

mofo (MOOF)
Malagasy bread.

mofo gasy (MOOF gash)
Malagasy bread made from a batter of sweetened rice flour.

ombiasy (om-bi-ASH)
Traditional healer.

paella
Seasoned rice with shrimp and chicken.

parique (pa-REEK)
Snack made from peanuts, rice, and sugar.

pousse-pousse (POOSS-POOSS)
Cart for passengers or goods, pulled by a man.

ranovola (RAHN-o-VOOL)
Water boiled with the crusty residue in the rice pot.

rougaille (roo-GUY)
Sauce made from tomatoes, ginger, onions, lemons, and hot peppers.

sodina (so-DEEN)
Traditional Malagasy flute.

taxi-brousse (tak-see-BROOS)
a minibus

tsingy (TSING-i)
Sharp limestone pinnacles.

valiha (va-LEE-a)
Musical instrument resembling a zither.

vintana (vin-TARN)
Person's fortune, fate, destiny.

FOR FURTHER INFORMATION

BOOKS

Berens, Ken and Keith Barnes. *Wildlife of Madagascar*. Princeton, NJ: Princeton University Press, 2016.

Chapple Wright, Patricia. *For the Love of Lemurs: My Life in the Wilds of Madagascar*. New York: Lantern Books, 2016.

Jolly, Alison and Hilary Bradt. *Thank You, Madagascar: The Conservation Diaries of Alison Jolly*. London: Zed Books, 2015.

Kabana, Joni. *Torina's World: A Child's Life in Madagascar*. Portland, OR: Arnica Publishing, 2007.

Lonely Planet and Emilie Filou. *Lonely Planet Madagascar*.

Tyson, Peter. *The Eight Continent: Life, Death, and Discovery in the Lost World of Madagascar*. New York: Harper Perennial, 2001; Chalfont St. Peter, UK: Bradt Travel Guides, 2013.

ONLINE

BBC News. Country Profile: Madagascar. http://www.bbc.com/news/world-africa-13861843

Central Intelligence Agency. The World Factbook. https://www.cia.gov/library/publications/the-world-factbook/geos/ma.html

Lonely Planet. Madagascar. https://www.lonelyplanet.com/madagascar

Trip Savvy. Madagascar Travel Guide: Essential Facts and Information. https://www.tripsavvy.com/madagascar-travel-guide-1454399

US Department of State. Madagascar. https://www.state.gov/p/af/ci/ma

FILMS AND VIDEOS

David Attenborough's Madagascar. http://www.bbc.co.uk/nature/collections/p00db3n8

Island of Lemurs. Warner Bros., 2014.

Madagascar. Vision Films, 2015.

The Enchanted Island, Madagascar: The Living Edens. Reader's Digest - ABC/Kane Productions, 1998.

MUSIC

A World Out of Time: Henry Kaiser and David Lindley in Madagascar. Shanachie, 1992.

Malagasy Guitar, D'Gary: Music from Madagascar. Shanachie, 1993.

Rough Guide to the Music of Madagascar. Various artists. World Music Network, 2005.

BIBLIOGRAPHY

Banka, Guifty, and Borghild Berge. "Malagasy Women Wounded by Child Marriage and its Aftermath." United Nations Population Fund, October 10, 2012. http://www.unfpa.org/news/malagasy-women-wounded-child-marriage-and-its-aftermath

BBC News. "Madagascar president forced out." March 17, 2009. http://news.bbc.co.uk/2/hi/africa/7948196.stm

CIA World Factbook. Madagascar. https://www.cia.gov/library/publications/the-world-factbook/geos/ma.html

Encyclopaedia Britannica. Madagascar. https://www.britannica.com/place/Madagascar

Ford, Peter. "Madagascar skirted famine—barely. Now, it's boosting resilience before drought returns." *The Christian Science Monitor*, July 25, 2017. https://www.csmonitor.com/World/Africa/2017/0725/Madagascar-skirted-famine-barely.-Now-it-s-boosting-resilience-before-drought-returns

Lykke Lind, Peter. "The bitter taste of Madagascar vanilla." Al Jazeera, February 19, 2017. http://www.aljazeera.com/indepth/features/2017/01/bitter-taste-madagascar-vanilla-170131073036652.html

Mada Magazine. http://www.madamagazine.com/en

Nour, Nawal M. "Health Consequences of Child Marriage in Africa." *Emerging Infectious Diseases*, November 2006. https://www.ncbi.nlm.nih.gov/pmc/articles/PMC3372345

UNFPA. "Profiles of 10 Countries With the Highest Rates of Child Marriage, Madagascar." *Marrying Too Young—End Child Marriage*. UNFPA 2012. http://www.unfpa.org/sites/default/files/jahia-publications/documents/publications/2012/ChildMarriage_8_annex1_indicator-definition.pdf

Vazaha Gasy. https://vazahagasy.wordpress.com

WildMadagascar.org. http://www.wildmadagascar.org

INDEX

INDEX